S0-BYQ-573

The Age of Exploration

Andrew A. Kling

LUCENT BOOKS
A part of Gale, Cengage Learning

GALE
CENGAGE Learning·

Detroit • New York • San Francisco • New Haven, Conn • Waterville, Maine • London

GALE
CENGAGE Learning™

© 2013 Gale, Cengage Learning

ALL RIGHTS RESERVED. No part of this work covered by the copyright herein may be reproduced, transmitted, stored, or used in any form or by any means graphic, electronic, or mechanical, including but not limited to photocopying, recording, scanning, digitizing, taping, Web distribution, information networks, or information storage and retrieval systems, except as permitted under Section 107 or 108 of the 1976 United States Copyright Act, without the prior written permission of the publisher.

Every effort has been made to trace the owners of copyrighted material.

LIBRARY OF CONGRESS CATALOGING-IN-PUBLICATION DATA

Kling, Andrew A., 1961-
  The age of exploration / by Andrew A. Kling.
    p. cm. -- (World history)
  Includes bibliographical references and index.
  ISBN 978-1-4205-0930-4 (hardcover)
  1. Discoveries in geography--Juvenile literature. 2. Explorers--Juvenile literature. I. Title.
  G175.K55 2013
  910.9--dc23
                                                      2012037342

Lucent Books
27500 Drake Rd.
Farmington Hills, MI 48331

ISBN-13: 978-1-4205-0930-4
ISBN-10: 1-4205-0930-6

Printed in the United States of America
1 2 3 4 5 6 7 16 15 14 13 12

Contents

Foreword

Each year, on the first day of school, nearly every history teacher faces the task of explaining why his or her students should study history. Many reasons have been given. One is that lessons exist in the past from which contemporary society can benefit and learn. Another is that exploration of the past allows us to see the origins of our customs, ideas, and institutions. Concepts such as democracy, ethnic conflict, or even things as trivial as fashion or mores, have historical roots.

Reasons such as these impress few students, however. If anything, these explanations seem remote and dull to young minds. Yet history is anything but dull. And therein lies what is perhaps the most compelling reason for studying history: History is filled with great stories. The classic themes of literature and drama—love and sacrifice, hatred and revenge, injustice and betrayal, adversity and overcoming adversity—fill the pages of history books, feeding the imagination as well as any of the great works of fiction do.

The story of the Children's Crusade, for example, is one of the most tragic in history. In 1212 Crusader fever hit Europe. A call went out from the pope that all good Christians should journey to Jerusalem to drive out the hated Muslims and return the city to Christian control. Heeding the call, thousands of children made the journey. Parents bravely allowed many children to go, and entire communities were inspired by the faith of these small Crusaders. Unfortunately, many boarded ships were captained by slave traders, who enthusiastically sold the children into slavery as soon as they arrived at their destination. Thousands died from disease, exposure, and starvation on the long march across Europe to the Mediterranean Sea. Others perished at sea.

Another story, from a modern and more familiar place, offers a soul-wrenching view of personal humiliation but also the ability to rise above it. Hatsuye Egami was one of 110,000 Japanese Americans sent to internment camps during World War II. "Since yesterday we Japanese have ceased to be human beings," he wrote in his diary. "We are numbers. We are no longer Egamis, but the number 23324. A tag with that number is on every trunk, suitcase and bag. Tags, also, on our breasts." Despite such dehumanizing treatment, most internees worked hard to control their bitterness. They created workable communities inside the camps and demonstrated again and again their loyalty as Americans.

These are but two of the many stories from history that can be found in the pages of the Lucent Books World History series. All World History titles rely on sound research and verifiable evidence, and all give students a clear sense of time, place, and chronology through maps and timelines as well as text.

All titles include a wide range of authoritative perspectives that demonstrate the complexity of historical interpretation and sharpen the reader's critical thinking skills. Formally documented quotations and annotated bibliographies enable students to locate and evaluate sources, often instantaneously via the Internet, and serve as valuable tools for further research and debate.

Finally, Lucent's World History titles present rousing good stories, featuring vivid primary source quotations drawn from unique, sometimes obscure sources such as diaries, public records, and contemporary chronicles. In this way, the voices of participants and witnesses as well as important biographers and historians bring the study of history to life. As we are caught up in the lives of others, we are reminded that we too are characters in the ongoing human saga, and we are better prepared for our own roles.

1488
Portuguese mariner Bartolomeu Dias sails around the southern cape of Africa.

1492
Italian explorer Christopher Columbus, under the Spanish flag, reaches the Bahamas Islands, Cuba, and Hispaniola.

1463
The Inca in Peru conquer the neighboring Chimu Empire, spreading their dominion along the northwest coast of South America.

1434
Portuguese mariner Gil Eanes succeeds in navigating around Africa's legendary Cape Bojador.

1380   1420   1460   1500   1540

1498
Portuguese explorer Vasco da Gama rounds Africa and reaches the Indian port of Calicut.

1521
Spanish conquistador Hernán Cortés and his allies defeat the Aztec Empire in Mexico. Ferdinand Magellan arrives in the Philippines.

1439
Johannes Gutenberg develops movable-type printing, revolutionizing the creation and production of books.

1535
French explorer Jacques Cartier reaches the sites of present-day Quebec City and Montreal in Canada.

1541
Spanish conquistador Hernando de Soto sights the Mississippi River. Spanish conquistador Francisco Vásquez de Coronado reaches present-day Kansas.

the Age of Exploration

1543
Nicolaus Copernicus publishes his theory that the earth and the other planets revolve around the sun.

1644
The Ming dynasty in China falls to Manchu invaders from Mongolia.

1654
The English seize the island of Jamaica from Spain.

1685
Classical composer Johann Sebastian Bach is born in Germany.

1687
René-Robert Cavelier, Sieur de La Salle, reaches the mouth of the Mississippi River.

1550	1600	1650	1700	1750

1579
Francis Drake arrives in England after a two-year-long voyage around the world.

1611
Henry Hudson and others are marooned in Hudson Bay, Canada.

1631
Thomas James and Luke Foxe explore Hudson Bay.

1641
The rulers of Japan institute policies that expel and ban foreigners from Japan.

1700
The Cascadia earthquake occurs off the coast of the Pacific Northwest and generates a tsunami that strikes Japan.

1684
The branch of mathematics known as calculus is developed by both Gottfried Leibniz and Isaac Newton (pictured).

Marco Polo and Prester John

At the start of the fourteenth century, life for the people of Europe was much as it had been for hundreds of years. Although many of the place names on the geographical landscape, such as lakes, rivers, and mountains, would be familiar to modern observers, the political landscape was much different. Individuals usually thought of themselves as citizens of a particular town or region. The seeds of the modern nations of England and France were already growing; however, the Iberian Peninsula, home to modern-day Portugal and Spain, was ruled by small kingdoms such as Castile, Navarre, and Aragon and was also home to Muslim settlers from North Africa. The Italian Peninsula was even more fragmented, with a variety of small kingdoms in the north and south. The central part of the peninsula was ruled directly by the pope and the Christian Church in Rome. Additionally, cities such as Genoa and Venice ruled themselves and were becoming important trading centers for goods entering and leaving Europe.

This trade, particularly with markets in the Middle East, enabled wealthy Europeans to purchase exotic items such as silks from China, carpets woven in Persia, and spices such as nutmeg, pepper, and cloves from mysterious places called Ceylon and Java. The Europeans purchased these goods through merchants in Middle Eastern towns such as Alexandria (in modern-day Egypt) or Damascus (in modern-day Syria). Muslim rulers in the region refused to allow Europeans to travel the overland routes to Persia and China or to sail from the ports on the Red Sea that would enable them to voyage to the far-off markets. This meant that European traders were obliged to pay whatever prices the merchants demanded for these luxury goods.

Then, for a brief period, the overland routes opened. Islamic power receded as the Mongol Empire expanded from China across Asia all the way to modern-day Iraq. The Mongols encouraged trade among nations, and from roughly 1250 to 1350, enterprising Italian merchants led overland caravans along the route known as the Silk Road to trading centers in India and China. The European traders were often away from home for years at a time. But when they came home, they brought back exotic goods rarely seen in Europe. They returned with manufactured goods such as porcelain wares or gems such as rubies and emeralds. They also returned with tales of fascinating and far-off lands and the people who lived there.

Two of these traders were brothers Niccolò and Maffeo Polo, from the city of Venice. They made a tremendously profitable journey to Mongol Asia that lasted nine years (1260–1269), during which they reached the court of the ruler Kublai Khan at his capital, Peking (modern-day Beijing, China). Upon their return to Venice, they outfitted a second expedition and this time took along Niccolò's son, seventeen-year-old Marco.

Marco Polo's name is legendary and has become synonymous with adventure and travel to distant lands. Yet it was due to a naval battle between rivals Venice and Genoa that Marco Polo's story survives to this day. Taken prisoner by the victorious Genoese, Polo became friends with another prisoner named Rustichello. Rustichello listened with fascination to Polo's tales of twenty-four years away from Europe, his service to the khan, and his adventures across the expanses of Asia. Around 1300 Rustichello's accounts of Marco Polo's adventures appeared in a book written in French, titled *Livres des merveilles du monde* ("Books of Marvels of the World"). This was an era when books were rare, because each new copy had to be written and illustrated by hand, but within a few decades Marco Polo's name was known throughout Europe, and his adventures had been translated into several languages, including Latin, Italian, and English.

The Mongol Empire receded, and Muslim power returned to cut off the trade routes. The tales of Marco Polo became even more fascinating and legendary. By 1400 Europeans no longer traveled beyond the Mediterranean Sea. The lands beyond became home to mythical sights and mysterious people, while eyewitness tales became more fantastical with each telling as they were passed down the generations and no new travelers added their own sagas. Perhaps just as importantly, especially to aspiring entrepreneurs, these lands were the source of untold treasures. The Muslim-controlled lands, however, lay in between.

In the face of Islamic power and expansion, Christians revived the legend of Prester John. As early as the twelfth century, stories began to circulate in Europe of a man who was king of an empire somewhere in the mystical lands beyond the Middle East that Europeans called the Indies. His realm

This illustration depicts Marco Polo setting out from Venice with his father and uncle to reach Kublai Khan in Mongol Asia. Polo became famous after accounts of his journeys appeared in the Books of Marvels of the World *around 1300.*

was surrounded but unconquered by Muslims. Prester John was a Christian warrior as well, supposedly descended from the race of the Three Wise Men who had attended the birth of Jesus Christ. Around 1165 an amazing document appeared in Europe, purportedly written by Prester John and addressed to two European kings. It described his kingdom in great detail and offered his services to help drive the Muslims from the Christian holy lands in the Middle East. According to historian Daniel J. Boorstin:

> Scholars have never established who really wrote the letter, where or why. We do know that it was a forgery, though we do not know in which language it was origi-

nally written. "Prester John's Letter" enjoyed enormous popularity across Europe. More than one hundred Latin manuscript editions have appeared, besides numerous others in Italian, German, English, Serbian, Russian, and Hebrew.[1]

Generations of Europeans hoped that Prester John was real and that someday they could unite with him against the Muslims. Religious leaders hoped that with his help they could expand Christianity. Enterprising merchants hoped that with his help they could reopen the trade routes to the Indies. As the fifteenth century dawned, both religious and economic aspirations led to a series of daring enterprises that not only expanded European horizons beyond the Mediterranean Sea, but literally changed the world forever.

Chapter One

Conquering the "Sea of Darkness"

For Europeans at the start of the fifteenth century, the world was centered on the Mediterranean Sea. Mariners had been sailing it since before recorded history, with the knowledge of islands, rocks, and shoals passed down from generation to generation by hands-on experience. Although printed charts of the Mediterranean, documenting entrances to harbors and dangerous coastlines, had existed for decades, the largely illiterate community of mariners preferred experience over written charts. Today historians recognize that these charts played an important role in world history beyond the Mediterranean.

Until the fifteenth century, European geography—the science of depicting landforms on a map—was heavily influenced by Christian thought. For example, there was a belief that an impassable fiery zone at the equator existed to the south of their known world. Below that were the Antipodes, in which every-

thing, they believed, was upside down. The theologians argued that because Noah's Ark came to rest north of the equator, no living creature could have reached the Antipodes, and if any had survived the Great Flood described in the Bible, they surely would not be among the descendants of Adam and Eve. Famous Christian philosophers such as Saint Augustine (A.D. 354–A.D. 430) and Saint Boniface (circa A.D. 675–A.D. 754) argued that the world was a flat disk. Few disputed their assertions. Consequently, for centuries maps created in Europe depicted a world centered on the Mediterranean that historians today call T-O maps.

The T-O Map

In a T-O map, east was placed at the top, representing the direction of the rising sun. The world was depicted as a circle surrounded by water (the O). A T-shaped flow of water divided the lands, which, according to geographical researcher and author Toby Lester, represented three bodies of water: the Mediterranean, separating Europe from Africa; the River Nile, believed to separate Africa from Asia; and the River Don in Russia, separating Europe from Asia.[2] Later T-O maps placed the revered city of Jerusalem in the center and included cities and regions. But the encircling ocean remained.

In the late fourteenth century, however, maps created in Europe began to change. This coincided with the rediscovery of works by ancient Greek mathematicians and philosophers. They had believed that the world was actually a sphere and theorized that there were undiscovered lands in the Antipodes. These challenges to established Christian thought led many Europeans to imagine what might exist beyond their

The T-O maps placed east, the direction of the rising sun, at the top. From Europe, therefore, Asia is shown at the top of the map. The world is depicted as a circle surrounded by water.

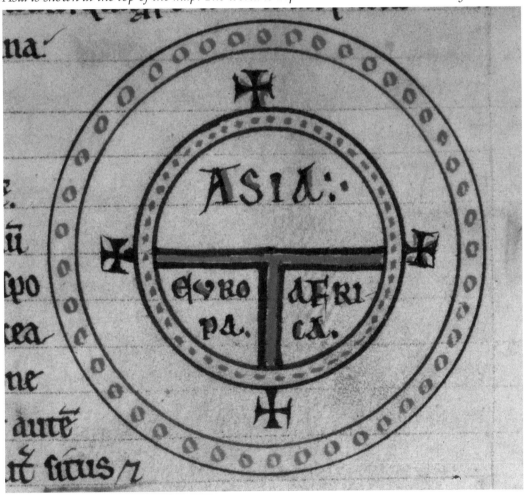

known world. The first expeditions beyond the lands on the T-O maps were led by men from the small nation of Portugal. Starting in the early 1400s, they began to expand the boundaries of navigation and geography in order to help advance their nation. And it all began with the third son of the Portuguese king, a prince named Henry.

Prince Henry the Navigator

Henry was born in 1394 and was the third son of Portugal's King John I and his English wife, Philippa of Lancaster. Portugal was newly independent, as Henry's father had secured Portugal's independence from the kingdom of Castile in 1385 with the aid of English arms. Since then Portugal had been at peace with its neighbors, and in 1411 John signed a long-term peace treaty with Castile.

Such peace was rare among European nations. This was an age in which kings and queens were continually challenged by invaders or insiders. For example, the Hundred Years' War, a conflict between England and France, raged on and off from 1337 to 1453. This was also an age in which young men, particularly princes, were expected to prove their adulthood through accomplishments on the battlefield, or in times of peace, in tournaments that featured jousting and other forms of mock combat. John planned a year-long tournament to commemorate the peace treaty with Castile, but Henry and his older brothers suggested an alternative to such an expensive affair. Instead of the mock combat of a tournament, they proposed an attack on Muslim territory.

Their target was Ceuta on the North African coast. The town sits on a peninsula that juts out from modern-day Morocco into the Strait of Gibraltar. In Henry's day it was a vibrant trading post where African caravans brought valuable goods from faraway lands. Henry and his older brothers felt that taking Ceuta from the Muslims would have two main benefits. It would enable Portugal to profit from the trade of goods, enriching the nation's treasury. Additionally, it would provide an opportunity for Henry and his brothers to prove themselves in battle. John agreed to the venture, and plans moved forward for the invasion of Ceuta.

The Lessons of Ceuta

The invasion took place in August 1415. The battle was one-sided and short-lived. The Portuguese conquered Ceuta within a day. Henry saw firsthand the riches that passed through the trading center. According to Boorstin:

> The loot in Ceuta was the freight delivered by the caravans that had been arriving there from Saharan Africa in the south and from the Indies in the east. In addition to the [everyday] essentials of life— wheat, rice, and salt—the Portuguese found exotic stores of pepper, cinnamon, cloves, ginger and other spices. Ceutan houses were hung with rich tapestries and carpeted with Oriental rugs. All in addition to the usual booty of gold and silver and jewels.[3]

The Revival of Ptolemy

As early as the fifth century B.C., several Greek mathematicians and geographers had theorized that the world was a sphere. To them the scientific evidence was irrefutable. For example, by measuring the length of shadows the sun cast at various locations and by using the distances between these locations and applying trigonometry, mathematicians were able to demonstrate that the earth was round. Men such as Erastothenes, Hipparchus, and Ptolemy had also created a grid system to map the earth (a precursor to modern latitude and longitude).

This knowledge was lost to western Europe for nearly one thousand years, because few people, even the most highly educated, could read Greek. After a copy of Ptolemy's work was translated into Latin in the late 1300s, western Europeans rediscovered the works of the ancient Greeks, and the science of geography was revitalized.

Ptolemy also acknowledged that undiscovered lands might exist beyond the world he knew. For example, he believed that Africa extended below the equator but was connected to a vast southern continent that joined eastern Asia, which effectively encircled today's Indian Ocean and the China Sea. In the new Latin versions of his maps, this area was labeled *Terra Incognita*, or "Unknown Land."

Soon trade ground to a halt. Muslim caravans began to bypass Ceuta to avoid its Christian occupiers. From the traders and merchants who remained, Henry learned all he could about the vast inland trade network. He realized that Portugal had an untapped advantage over its neighbors. Because it had no ports on the Mediterranean, it was at the far western end of trade routes for goods from faraway markets. It did, however, possess a long coastline and numerous harbors that faced the open Atlantic Ocean. Henry believed that Portugal's fate lay in that direction. In fact, according to a fifteenth-century historian, Henry believed that his own fate lay that way as well. His astrologer had predicted that "this prince was bound to engage in great and noble conquests, and above all was he bound to attempt the discovery of things which were hidden from other men, and secret."[4] He believed that it was his destiny to discover new lands that would enrich his nation, to gather new information about Muslim power, to expand Christianity by converting new peoples, and perhaps even to make contact with the famous Prester John.

Upon his return from Ceuta, Henry moved to Sagres, on the far southwestern tip of Portugal, where he established a center for navigation. He understood that new and unknown lands could be discovered only by clearly establishing the boundaries of the old and known lands. From Sagres he began to research how to venture into the unknown.

Gathering Information

Henry was determined to fulfill his destiny, but he was also determined to do so as safely as possible. He invited a wide variety of experts in the fields of navigation, mapmaking, and shipbuilding to work in Sagres. He showed a remark-

Portugal's Henry the Navigator was chiefly responsible for that country's Age of Exploration.

able lack of prejudice among men of his day by encouraging input from a wide variety of faiths, skills, and nationalities. For example, he hired Jehuda Cresques, a famous Jewish cartographer from the Spanish island of Majorca, to teach mapmaking at Sagres. He also collected the latest maps and navigational records. When his brother Pedro went on a tour throughout the royal capitals of Europe, he returned with manuscripts and records of a number of famous travelers, including Marco Polo.

Contributions also arrived from Italian, German, and Scandinavian mariners and from Muslim traders based in North Africa and the Middle East. They shared their charts and knowledge of wind patterns and currents, the Azores and Canary Islands in the Atlantic Ocean, and news of markets beyond Africa's Sahara Desert that Europeans had never seen.

Each piece of data enabled Henry and his team to assemble geographic facts that were free from the beliefs of Christian dogma. Yet this knowledge was only part of the challenge. Being able to get to new lands and to return safely was another. To that end, Henry worked with Portuguese craftspeople and mariners to develop a new type of ship. They called it the caravel.

The Caravel

Henry wanted his sailors to have vessels that were small and maneuverable. Large ships with square sails, such as those used by traders in the Mediterranean, were best suited for carrying large cargoes and for sailing with the wind. In other words, they were most efficient when the wind came over the stern, or back end of the ship. Henry felt that his mariners would benefit from ships that could maneuver when the wind came from the side as well as from the stern.

Two ship designs seemed particularly valuable. Both used triangular sails rather than square ones. An Arab coastal vessel called a *caravos* had been used since ancient times and could carry crews of up to thirty men and a substantial cargo. A smaller, more maneuverable type, called the caravela, was used in Portugal's Douro River. Henry's shipbuilders combined features of both to create a new class of vessel they called the caravel.

The first caravels were approximately 70 feet (21.3m) in length and about 25 feet (7.6m) in width. Each caravel carried two or three triangular sails. The vessel could comfortably accommodate a crew of twenty, who usually slept in the open on the top deck. It had enough cargo space to carry supplies for an extended voyage of several weeks. Its shallow draft meant it could be easily sailed close to shore without worrying about running aground. The caravel also had excellent maneuverability, surpassing other designs of the day in the ability to make progress against headwinds.

Between 1424 and 1433 Henry sent mariners from Portugal's Atlantic ports southward along the northwestern coast of Africa. While the advanced design of the caravel worked well at sea, none of the expeditions furthered his knowledge of the area. All returned without having passed beyond a landmark the Portuguese called Cape Bojador, or the "Bulging Cape."

Cape Bojador

Cape Bojador lies along the coast of modern-day Western Sahara. On modern maps it does not seem like an imposing geographic challenge, yet its reputation was known far and wide among European mariners. Among the challenges were a strong coastal current that pushed vessels south toward the cape; at the cape this current met ocean currents that flowed north, which created treacherous whirlpools. The sea crashed against the cape's overhanging cliffs, sending chunks of red sand tumbling into the waves. Exceedingly shallow waters stretched over 3 miles (4.8km) from shore. An unseen reef extended out to sea, and when waves broke against it, even on calm days, spouts of water created high, foamy clouds that made it look like the water was steaming. Large schools of small fish such as sardines were pushed to the surface by larger fish feeding below; the smaller fish thrashed the water, adding to the impression that the sea was boiling. Each of these obstacles seemed to the mariners to appear suddenly and without warning, giving them little time to navigate around them.

The mariners also noted the coastline was oddly deserted; no one seemed to live there. Hot desert air blew over them, driven by offshore winds. These conditions added to the sailors' impression that they had reached the proverbial gates of

The Sea of Darkness

The open ocean beyond the Mediterranean Sea's Strait of Gibraltar was a source of mystery and danger. European mariners sailed to ports in the British Isles and along the Baltic and North Sea coasts, but they were rarely out of sight of land. They sailed close to the shore, navigating mainly by landward features that they could see from their ships. Those who survived these voyages shared tales of being caught in dangerous storms that blew in from the open ocean and of long, dark, cold nights on the seas. Those who did not survive were remembered by their colleagues, who imagined a wide variety of reasons for their demise.

Muhammad al-Idrisi, a twelfth-century Muslim geographer, summed up the prevailing attitude when he wrote, "No one knows what exists beyond this sea. . . . No one has been able to learn for certain, because of the dangers to navigation caused by the impenetrable darkness, the great waves, the frequent storms and violent winds, and the multitude of sea monsters." The Atlantic Ocean beyond the Mediterranean was therefore known as the "Green Sea of Gloom" or the *Sea of Darkness*.

Quoted in Toby Lester. *The Fourth Part of the World.* New York: Free Press, 2009, p. 31.

Sea monsters were believed to attack ships that ventured into the Sea of Darkness.

hell at end of the world. The fifteenth-century chronicler Gomes Eanes de Zurara recounted that mariners believed that "the currents are so terrible that no ship having once passed the Cape, will ever be able to return.... These mariners of ours ... [were] threatened not only by fear but by its shadow, whose great deceit was the cause of very great expenses."[5] The conditions seemed to support centuries of Christian thought and to present tangible evidence of the dangers of the "Sea of Darkness" that supposedly encircled the world.

Henry realized his sailors could not conquer the physical barriers of Cape Bojador until they had conquered the mental barriers first. Over a dozen expeditions returned with the belief that the cape represented the edge of the world. In 1433 Henry selected Gil Eanes, one of the navigators trained at Sagres, to conquer Cape Bojador, but Eanes returned without having done so. The following year Eanes made a second attempt. This time, however, he sailed westward into the Atlantic Ocean before turning south. In so doing he discovered that he had passed beyond Cape Bojador. When he made landfall south of the cape, he found the land was desolate, but it was certainly not the end of the world. With this single accomplishment, Eanes broke through the climate of fear surrounding Cape Bojador, and he opened the door for further Portuguese exploration along the African coast.

Beyond Cape Bojador

Following Eanes's successful voyage, Henry sent further expeditions along the coast beyond Cape Bojador. Eanes's next voyage, in 1435, sailed an additional 50 leagues, or 150 miles (241km), south. When he and his crew landed on the shore, they saw footprints of camels and men but did not make contact with the inhabitants. With each succeeding year Portuguese ships explored farther down the coast. Henry encouraged the explorers to sail into unknown waters, as long as they could return safely.

With these early efforts, Henry implemented a requirement that became an important precedent in the Age of Exploration. He ordered all ships' captains to keep accurate logs of how far they had sailed and to make observations of the coastline and the surrounding land. These records provided Henry with vital feedback, which he understood was essential in exploration. The captains' documented evidence not only supported their claims of new distances traveled and new lands sighted, it also enabled better preparation for later expeditions.

One important piece of feedback concerned navigation in these unknown waters. The farther south the Portuguese traveled, the more difficult it was to determine the ship's location. Measuring latitude, their distance north of the equator, was achieved by measuring the angle of the sun above the horizon at noon. On land, scientists used a device called an astrolabe to measure latitude, but the device was fragile and unsuited for use on board the unsteady deck of a ship. Instead, Henry's navigators used a simpler wooden device called a cross-staff. The cross-staff consisted of two

Portuguese Explorer Routes

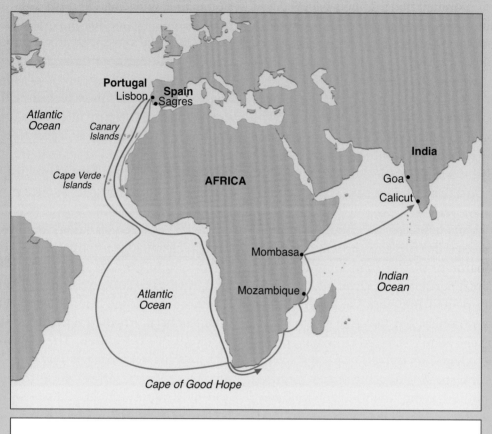

Voyages sponsored by Henry the Navigator (1418–1460)
Dias (1487–1488)
da Gama (1497–1498)

Taken from: www.classzone.com/cz/books/ms.wcg_survey/resources/images.

pieces: a stick marked with graduated measurements and a shorter crosspiece that slid along it. A mariner held it to his eye with the crosspiece perpendicular to the horizon. He then slid the crosspiece along the stick until the bottom edge appeared to touch the horizon and the top edge caught the sun. The location of the crosspiece on the staff's measurements enabled him to measure how high the sun was above the horizon, and with information from a trigonometry table, he then determined the ship's latitude. The cross-staff was less accurate than the astrolabe, but it withstood the rigors of ocean travel.

By the early 1440s Portugal's voyages beyond Cape Bojador had traveled along relatively barren coastlines. So far, the nation had little to show for the expense of Henry's expeditions. Public criticism of his explorations began to grow.

Economic Benefits

Widespread public complaints of Henry's expensive ventures changed when Eanes returned from a voyage in August 1444. He had explored an area called Capo Blanco (in modern-day Mauritania) and returned with a cargo that helped to change perceptions of African exploration. Eanes's ships brought two hundred African men, women, and children, who were sold into slavery. The profits from the sale, along with the prospect of new populations to be converted to Christianity, turned public criticisms into accolades.

The following year Dinis Dias rounded a point called Cabo Verde (today's Cap Vert in modern-day Senegal) at the westernmost point of Africa. Soon each voyage returned with valuable cargoes of pepper, ivory, gold, and other precious commodities, as well as more slaves. Before the decade ended, twenty-five caravels a year were engaged in trade along what was called the Guinea Coast. At the same time, Henry's captains continued recording their discoveries. One, Alvise da Cadamosto, traveled up the Senegal and Gambia Rivers and returned with enthralling observations of local customs and curious animals such as elephants and hippopotami.

Henry died in 1460, having never joined his mariners on their voyages of exploration and discovery. His contributions to the sciences of geography and navigation, however, laid the foundation for future explorations. In recognition of his pioneering efforts, biographers in the nineteenth century gave him the nickname "the Navigator," which endures to this day.

Padrãos Mark the Way

Following Henry's death, generations of Portuguese mariners continued to push back the limits of the blank areas on Ptolemy's maps that were labeled *Terra Incognita* (or, "Unknown Land"). The leadership mantle was taken up by Henry's nephew, King Afonso V. In 1469 Afonso granted a contract to Fernão Gomes, which pioneered the practice of government and private business working together toward a common goal. Gomes, a wealthy businessperson, agreed to explore an additional 300 miles (483km) of the African coast each year for the next five years in exchange for a monopoly of the Guinea trade. The Portuguese nation, in return, received a share of the profits.

As the Portuguese sailed farther into the unknown, around the western bulge of the African continent, they left stone markers, called *padrãos*, on coastal landmarks to mark the farthest point of each expedition. Some in Portugal believed that the voyagers were placing the markers across the southern reaches of the continent. Others believed they were marking their passage through

Ibn Majid

Shihab al-Din Ahmad ibn Majid was born into a seafaring family in the 1430s and became an accomplished navigator as a teenager at a time when Muslim fleets controlled the Indian Ocean. His work *The Book of Profitable Things Concerning the First Principles and Rules of Navigation*, written around 1490, demonstrated how to navigate using compasses and the stars and documented wind and ocean current conditions between Africa and India. It remained the standard for how to sail the Indian Ocean for over three hundred years.

In the 1920s a French historian theorized that Ibn Majid was the pilot hired by Vasco da Gama at the port of Malindi. Fifteenth-century Portuguese accounts say that the pilot da Gama hired was a "Moor from Guzerate" (in other words, a non-Caucasian from Gujurat in western India) who returned with the ships to Europe. More recent scholarship refutes this theory. Historian Sanjay Subrahmanyam notes, "Unless we wish to argue that Ibn Majid had in his [old age] taken on a Gujarti guise, visited Lisbon, and then said nothing of it in his writings, we shall have to bury the hypothesis once and for all, the more so since there is no indication that da Gama's (probably Gujarati) pilot ever returned to Asia."

Sanjay Subrahmanyam. *The Career and Legend of Vasco da Gama*. Cambridge: Cambridge University Press, 1997, p. 128.

a great "Gulf of Ethiopia" that nearly split the continent in two. According to some tales, ships could navigate the gulf almost to the eastern coast of Africa, where Prester John awaited them. This gulf even appeared on a document known today as the Catalan-Estense world map, which was drawn around 1450.

Gomes's sailors, however, discovered the map was wrong. According to geographical researcher and author Toby Lester, in 1474 "two of Fernão Gomes's sailors returned to Portugal with some disheartening news. After traveling along the bottom of the Western African can bulge for some 1,500 miles, they reported, they had arrived at a point (in present-day Cameroon) where the coast of Africa once again turned sharply to the south—and stretched out in that direction as far as the eye could see."[6]

When the contract with Gomes expired in 1474, Afonso transferred the trade monopoly to his own son, Prince John. By that time Gomes's ships had explored around the central western coast of Africa, into the Bight of Benin, and south across the equator. The distance they covered in five years equaled what Henry's navigators had achieved in thirty.

In 1482 Diogo Cão followed the west-facing coast as far as present-day Angola. Believing that he was about to round the southern tip of Africa, he returned with the great news, producing a chart of his findings to the king. Using this feedback, the Portuguese announced across Europe that their sailors had almost reached the tip of the continent. Unfortunately, the cape that Cão documented in his chart existed only in his imagination. He returned to the region in 1485 and sailed far beyond his previous journey, finding nothing but the arid coastline of present-day Namibia. He left a *padrão* and, according to Lester, "vanished from history"[7] after his expedition was lost at sea.

After Afonso's death in 1481, his son became King John II. The new king wanted to ensure that Portugal was the first to reach the southern tip of Africa. He carefully planned and organized a new expedition that was designed to range farther and to stay at sea longer than any previous attempt. This expedition's results, however, far exceeded the expectations of the king, the mariners, and the nation.

The Voyage of Bartolomeu Dias

In August 1487 a fleet of three ships set sail from Lisbon, Portugal, under the command of Bartolomeu Dias, a respected sea captain. Two caravels were accompanied by a larger ship laden with supplies to ensure a longer voyage than ever

before. Dias left the supply ship along the Namibian coast, passed Cão's last *padrão*, and kept going. Currents running north impeded the expedition's progress; westerly winds threatened to blow the ships ashore. On December 4, 1487, the fleet was hit by a large storm, and Dias ordered his ships to sail west, out to sea, to avoid wrecking on the coast. The storm lasted thirteen days, and the ships were blown to the south far beyond the sight of land. When the weather finally cleared, Dias sailed east, assuming they would eventually reach the coast.

Several days later, with no land sighted, Dias turned his ships north and discovered a coastline that traveled east and west, not north and south. In February 1488 they anchored briefly in a bay to take on water and food. They sailed 300 miles (483km) farther east, finding the coast now trended northeast. Dias wished to continue, believing that they would eventually reach the Indian Ocean, but after a meeting with his captains, he agreed to return to Portugal. They placed a *padrão* on a rocky headland on March 12, 1488, and turned back. Sailing close to the coast, they discovered what they had missed during the storm: a majestic and rocky headland jutting into the Atlantic Ocean near the southern tip of Africa's west coast. They erected a *padrão* at what they called the Cape of Storms and turned north. They eventually reunited with the supply ship and its crew, which they had left nine months earlier. The ship was in poor condition, so they burned it rather than try to sail it home.

Dias returned to Portugal in December 1488. The expedition had been gone more than sixteen months. Today historians believe that their first landfall was in Mossel Bay, South Africa; remains of their March 12, 1488, *padrão* have been found farther east, along Algoa Bay. Despite Dias's reckonings, John was

In August 1487 Bartolomeu Dias set sail from Portugal with three ships to explore the African coast. His explorations proved that Africa extended farther south than had been previously thought.

reluctant to believe that Dias had rounded Africa. Dias's report documented that Africa extended much farther south than anyone, including Cão, had anticipated. Even if Dias had rounded Africa, the journey turned out to be far longer and more treacherous than expected. The king, however, felt that Dias's discoveries were important enough that at least one geographic feature warranted a name change: He renamed the Cape of Storms the Cape of Good Hope. It represented the quiet optimism that a route around Africa to the Indies had indeed been found.

Vasco da Gama

Several years passed before Portugal was able to exploit the route that Dias had pioneered. John died in 1495. Political disputes over his successor and threats of war with Spain occupied the nation's attention. Eventually, John's successor, Manuel I, decided that Portugal should return to the high seas and proposed an expedition to voyage around Africa to bypass the overland trade routes controlled by the Muslims and their European partners in Venice and Genoa. The expedition's destination was a well-known Indian trading center called Calicut.

The king chose a sailor and diplomat named Vasco da Gama to lead this expedition. On July 8, 1497, da Gama left from Portugal with a fleet of four vessels, about 170 sailors, and enough provisions for three years. The fleet sailed almost due south into the Atlantic Ocean before turning east. It rounded the southern tip of Africa in November and sailed up the east coast of the continent, making several stops along the way in African ports. The Muslim leaders the Portuguese encountered were suspicious of their intentions, especially the farther north they sailed. At each stop, da Gama tried to hire an experienced sailor to serve as a pilot for their crossing of the Indian Ocean. In nautical terms a pilot is an individual with specialized knowledge of local waters, but the first pilots provided by the local leaders were, in Boorstin's words, "ignorant or treacherous."[8] Finally, at Malindi (in modern-day Kenya), da Gama hired a pilot who successfully guided the fleet across the Arabian Sea. The Portuguese arrived in Calicut on May 22, 1498.

"Greatly Rejoicing at Our Good Fortune"

Today the port of Calicut is the modern-day Indian city of Kozhikode. By 1498 Arab traders had been voyaging there for centuries to trade for spices, such as pepper and cardamom, and jewels, such as emeralds and rubies. The arrival of the Portuguese threatened to undermine their monopoly. Perhaps it was their influence that turned da Gama's negotiations for a trade agreement into a three-month marathon of discussions with the local ruler. Finally, in late August 1498, the Portuguese decided to leave. Da Gama did not record his thoughts of the voyage, but the memoir of one of his crew members, João da Sá, has survived. He wrote that da Gama and the other captains "agreed that, inasmuch that we had discovered the country we had come in search of, as also spices and precious stones, and it appeared impossible to establish cordial relations with the people, it would be as well to take our departure. We therefore set sail and left for Portugal, greatly rejoicing at our good fortune in having made so great a discovery."[9]

Although da Gama failed to secure a trade agreement, he was able to purchase a large cargo of spices before departing. The fleet endured a series of hardships on the way home, including contrary winds and more troubles with local Muslim leaders. Additionally, da Gama lost more than half of his crew to scurvy (brought on by lack of vitamin C in the diet). His fleet, reduced to two ships, returned to Lisbon in August 1499.

His return was met with great acclaim. One Italian chronicler wrote, "An enterprise has been carried out that arouses the admiration of the whole world. The spices that should, or used to, go to Cairo by way of the Red Sea are now carried to Lisbon."[10] Manuel wrote a letter to King Ferdinand and Queen Isabella of Spain, touting da Gama's achievements:

> Your Highnesses already know that we had ordered Vasco da Gama . . . with four vessels to make discoveries by sea, and that two years have now elapsed since their departure. . . . From a message which has now been brought to [me] by one of his captains, we learn that they did reach and discover India . . . [and]

that they entered and navigated its sea, finding large cities . . . and great populations, among whom is carried on all the trade in spices and precious stones, which are forwarded in ships . . . to Mecca, and thence to Cairo, whence they are dispersed throughout the world. . . . As we are aware that your Highnesses will hear of these things with much pleasure and satisfaction, we thought well to give this information.[11]

In the following years successively larger fleets followed da Gama's route to India. The new Portugal-to-India route was so successful that by 1503, the price of pepper in Lisbon was one-fifth of its cost in Venice. The Portuguese intrusion into the markets of Calicut, however, was only the beginning of their presence in the Indian Ocean.

The Portuguese in India

At the start of the sixteenth century, Portugal sent larger and larger fleets around Africa and into the Indian Ocean. For example, in 1505 Francisco de Almeida commanded a flotilla of more than twenty ships eastward. The flotilla established trading bases along the east coast of Africa and along the coast of India. Almeida's son Lourenço explored south to the island of Ceylon (today's Sri Lanka), which he discovered was the source of cinnamon.

These new fleets were sponsored by the Portuguese government and had the latest European innovations in sailing

Vasco da Gama (pictured) was sent by King Manuel I to lead an expedition of four ships around the bottom of Africa and then to India, where he landed in 1498.

vessels and armaments. Through superior firepower and intimidation, the Portuguese succeeded in breaking the Muslim monopoly on Indian trade. They seized and destroyed opposition trading vessels and imprisoned and executed those who opposed them. In 1509 Portuguese vessels under Almeida defeated a fleet of

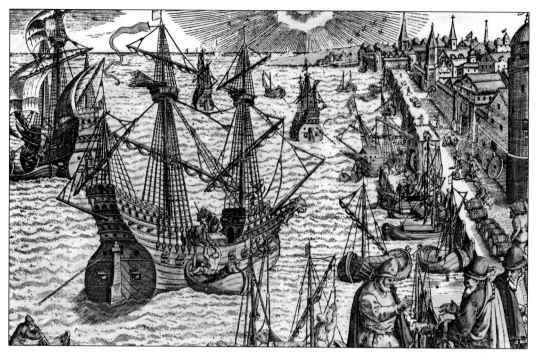

At the start of the sixteenth century, Portugal sent fleets of ships like these to establish trading colonies in India and thus break the Muslim monopoly on Indian trade.

Muslim, Indian, and European allies at the Battle of Diu along the northwestern Indian coast. Although the Portuguese were outnumbered more than ten to one in terms of ships, most of the Portuguese ships were advanced in design and heavily armed, whereas their opposition used smaller craft that had few cannons available. The victory gave the Portuguese control of the Indian Ocean.

In 1510 Afonso de Albuquerque conquered the Indian city of Goa, and over the next several years the Portuguese made it the center of their expanding Indian trade. There they heard amazing stories of a rich commercial center called Malacca. In 1511 Albuquerque led a fleet east across the Bay of Bengal to see if the tales of Malacca's riches were true.

The Riches of Malacca

When Albuquerque arrived in Malacca (in modern-day Malaysia) in 1511, the variety of goods available there stunned the Portuguese. One observer, Tomés Pires, said that there "you find what you want, and sometimes more than you are looking for. . . . Goods from all over the East are found here; goods from all over the West are sold here."[12] Traders arrived from ports the Portuguese already knew: Indians from Gujarat, Bengal, and Calicut; Africans from Mogadishu, Mombasa, and Malindi; and Arabians from Ormuz, Aden, and Socotra. There were also traders from places they did not know, such as modern-day Thailand and China. Cargoes of horses, dates, rice, wheat, soap, porcelain, pearls, sandalwood, cloves, and more changed hands in Malacca's markets.

The Portuguese wrested control of the city from the local rulers, and the wealth of trading goods started flowing back to Lisbon. Albuquerque and his men were fascinated by the extent of the network of trade that existed there. The following year he sent a portion of a map to Manuel that documented this network. He apologized that the full map was lost in a shipwreck but wrote that it had covered the Indian Ocean from Africa to Southeast Asia, including Java and Malacca, and showed the routes taken by navigators from all directions, including China. He maintained that the portion he was sending was "a very accurate and ascertained thing, because it is the real navigation, whence they come and whither they return."[13]

The trade network that the Portuguese found in Malacca inspired them to continue to explore. This time they turned north toward China.

China and Japan

When the Portuguese discovered that many Chinese goods flowed through Malacca, they investigated trading with China directly. Initially, they were rebuffed. They arrived in the port of Canton (modern-day Guangzhou) in 1517, but the Chinese emperor's representatives refused to meet with them. The Chinese sent a fleet to drive off the

The port of Malacca, Malaysia, in the sixteenth century was a prosperous center of trade where East met West. The Portuguese wrested control of the city from local rulers and directed trade profits to Portugal.

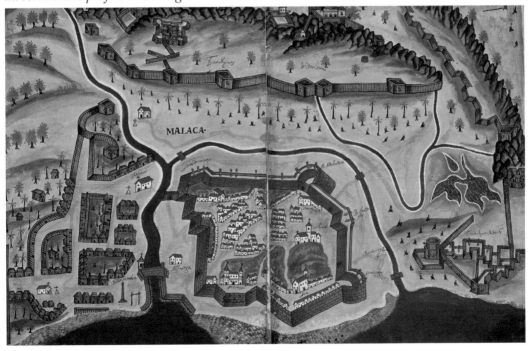

newcomers; it proved more powerful than the Portuguese expected, and the Europeans were defeated. The Portuguese, however, were undeterred and spent more than ten years in informal trade through a variety of Chinese ports. The Portuguese sailed along the coastline, searching for merchants who were willing to sell Chinese goods in defiance of the emperor's ban on foreign trade. The ban was eventually lifted in 1530, and the Portuguese received permission to establish a trading center in Macau in 1547.

In 1543 they opened a new market, completely by accident. In an incident reminiscent of Dias's storm-tossed encounter with the southern tip of Africa, a storm pushed a Portuguese ship bound for China to the north. When the storm abated, the ship made landfall, and purely by accident the crew discovered they were in yet another new land: Japan.

Since the days of Marco Polo, Japan had been a mythical land for Europeans. The Chinese and Polo had called it Cipangu, and it was said to be full of riches, particularly precious metals. At the time the Portuguese landed on the southern island of Tanegashima, Japanese traders had been banned from trading with China by the Chinese emperor. The Europeans served as intermediaries, and soon Portuguese vessels brought goods between China and Japan, with porcelain and silk traveling to the mainland in return for silver and copper.

The Spirit of Prince Henry the Navigator

By the end of the sixteenth century, Portuguese mariners and ships regularly visited ports from western Africa to southern Japan. In less than 150 years, the small European nation had changed the world as Europeans knew it. The successors to Prince Henry the Navigator's first pioneering mariners fostered connections with civilizations previously known only through legend. They charted routes to far-off lands and brought back knowledge of the planet that thrilled merchants and geographers alike. They had not filled in all of the terra incognita on Ptolemy's maps, but they had added greatly to the knowledge of previously unknown shorelines. Perhaps most importantly, they had consigned to the past the fear of sailing out of sight of land, and in so doing conquered the legendary Sea of Darkness.

These explorers were not alone in their pioneering work to reach the Indies, however. Before Dias returned from the tip of South Africa, other mariners wondered whether the Portuguese might succeed in their quest, and if they did, whether the route might be too long for practical purposes. One of these mariners was an Italian named Cristoforo Colombo. Today he is better known by the English form of his name in Latin: Christopher Columbus. He challenged the prevailing perceptions and ended up changing the history of the world.

Chapter Two

Columbus and the Conquistadores

As Portuguese mariners pushed along the coast of the African continent in the 1470s and 1480s, European engravers and printers included the latest discoveries on their newest maps. Starting with Ptolemy's designs, they added decorative touches to make their work stand out. For example, in 1482 a set of Ptolemy's maps was printed in Ulm, in present-day Germany. The Ulm edition continued to show the southern part of Africa attached to a great and as yet unknown southern continent that joined Southeast Asia to encircle the Indian Ocean. But around the edges of the map, the printers added twelve decorative heads with puffed cheeks, depicting directions of the winds. They were a whimsical addition to this colorful map that within a decade would be obsolete, thanks to the voyage of Bartolomeu Dias.

While these new maps played a vital role in the growing science of cartography in Europe, they lacked precise measurements. As far back as the ancient Greeks, scientists and geographers disagreed about how large the world actually was. The Greeks divided the planet's sphere into 360 degrees of longitude around the equator. Ptolemy believed that each degree of longitude at the equator was 50 miles (80.47km), making the earth 18,000 miles (roughly 29,000km) around. Additionally, he estimated that Asia stretched fully 180 degrees (half the globe) from east to west.

Today we know that each degree at the equator is 70 miles (112.65km), giving the earth a circumference of 25,200 miles (40,555km), and that Asia only stretches 130 degrees from east to west. Ptolemy had underestimated the size of the globe by more than 25 percent. Some observers believed it was even smaller than that. One of them was Christopher Columbus.

Columbus's Worldview

Columbus was born in 1451 in Genoa, in modern-day Italy. By the mid-1480s he was an experienced mariner and navigator who had sailed the Mediterranean and the Atlantic as far north as Great Britain and as far south as West Africa's Guinea Coast. These voyages inspired him to learn more about the world beyond Europe. He obtained a variety of books in several languages, including a copy of Marco Polo's travels in Latin, and made notes in their margins that recorded his ideas of the world.

Columbus became obsessed with the idea of traveling to the East Indies, China, and Japan. He argued that the earth was round and thus it was possible to reach China and Japan by sailing west.

He became obsessed with the idea of traveling to the legendary riches of the Indies of China and Japan. He used Marco Polo's terms *Cathay* and *Cipangu*, respectively, for them in his writings. He also formulated his own theory about the size of the earth. For example, when Columbus read a translation of the ninth-century Persian astronomer Alfraganus and his estimate of the size of the planet, he incorrectly assumed Alfraganus's measurements were in the Italian mile that Columbus knew, rather that the longer Arabic mile Alfraganus knew. According to historian Louis de Vorsey Jr., "In Columbus's world view the sphere of the earth was 10 percent smaller than Ptolemy thought it was."[14] Columbus's son Ferdinand wrote that his father believed "that a large part of this sphere had already been navigated and there remained to be discovered only the space which extended from the eastern end of [Asia] . . . eastward to the Cape Verde and Azores Islands, the westernmost land discovered."[15]

Columbus, therefore, argued that it should be possible to sail to Cathay and Cipangu from Europe by sailing west. He was willing to undertake the adventure, but he needed funding to make it happen.

Columbus requests financial aid for his expeditions from Queen Isabella and King Ferdinand of Spain. In 1491 they finally agreed to provide financing and ships for Columbus's expedition west.

Obtaining Royal Funding

In 1484 Columbus met with Portugal's King John II. He had sailed with Portuguese traders to Africa and valued their spirit of discovery, and he hoped the king would back his venture. He argued that Asia was much larger than anyone knew; instead of taking up 180 degrees of earth's surface, as Ptolemy claimed, he argued that it took up 225 degrees of it. Additionally, he believed Cipangu (Japan) would be found 30 degrees east of Cathay (China). His final calculations convinced him that it was a voyage of merely 2,400 miles (roughly 3,900km) from the Canary Islands (off the coast of northwestern Africa) to Cipangu.

The king was impressed by Columbus's presentation but politely turned him down. According to the sixteenth-century Portuguese chronicler João de Barros, the king's advisers "all considered the words of [Columbus] as vain, simply founded on imagination, or things like that Isle Cipango of Marco Polo."[16] Rejected by the Portuguese, Columbus spoke with Queen Isabella of Spain in 1486 but received no decision from her government for over a year. In 1488 Columbus returned to Portugal. He was in Lisbon when Dias returned with word that he had rounded the southern tip of Africa. Columbus was present as Dias documented his voyage before the king, and Columbus realized that there was no chance that Portugal would fund his enterprise. He returned to Spain to press his message with Isabella.

Several years passed before Columbus could speak again with Isabella and her husband, King Ferdinand. He met with them in late 1491 at Santa Fe in southern Spain. Ferdinand and Isabella believed that the expedition was possible but refused to meet Columbus's demands, such as a percentage of the profits on trade with the Indies and governorship over any new lands he might discover. As Columbus was leaving Santa Fe, the king and queen changed their minds. In the words of naval historian and Columbus scholar Samuel Eliot Morison:

Luis Santangel [Ferdinand's treasurer], called on the Queen the very day that Columbus left Santa Fe and urged her to meet Columbus's terms. The expedition, he pointed out, would not cost as much as a week's entertainment of a foreign prince. [Columbus] asked for honors . . . only in the event of success; and they would be a small price to pay for the discovery of new islands and a western route to the Indies. The Queen jumped at this. . . . A messenger overtook Columbus at a village four miles from Santa Fe, and brought him back.[17]

Months of preparation followed. Columbus's fleet consisted of three ships and approximately one hundred men. The largest vessel, the *Santa Maria*, was square-rigged and about 85 feet (26m) long. Next was the *Pinta*, a caravel of about 69 feet (21m); the smallest was the *Niña*, also a caravel, about 55 feet (17m). The ships departed from the Spanish port of Palos on August 1, 1492. After a stop for repairs in the Canary Islands, they set sail to the west into the open ocean.

"Tierra! Tierra!"

As Columbus ventured into the open Atlantic from the Canary Islands, he was reluctant to inform his men just how far he felt they had sailed. To this end, he maintained two log books; one had the official reckoning of distance covered each day, and the other had what he personally felt had been covered. The one he showed the crew always had the shorter distances. The sixteenth-century historian Bartolomé de Las Casas, who created a digest of this voyage from Columbus's now-lost log books, peppered his account with examples of this practice. For example, on the first day sailing west, "[Columbus] made fifteen leagues [45 miles or 72km] that day and decided to score up a smaller amount so that the crews should not take fright or lose courage if the voyage were long."[18] The next day Las Casas wrote that Columbus reckoned 60 leagues (180 miles or 290km) traveled but reported only 48 (144 miles or 232km). As it turned out, Columbus was overestimating the fleet's speed, and, in the words of Morison, "the 'false' reckoning was more nearly correct than the 'true'!"[19]

Regardless of the distances traveled, however, the crew began to grumble

Amerigo Vespucci

Amerigo Vespucci was a native of Florence, Italy, and worked in Spain as a merchant supplying food for ocean voyages, including Columbus's second voyage in 1493. In 1499 he sailed with a Spanish fleet that explored the South American coast as far south as the mouth of the Amazon River. Two years later he sailed with a Portuguese fleet that sailed for more than 2,500 miles (4,023km) along an unknown coast that traveled to the southwest.

The presence of this apparently large and previously unknown continent baffled and challenged mapmakers across Europe. They had to try to piece together where the explorers had been and then depict it accurately. Some believed this landmass was part of far eastern Asia as depicted by Ptolemy. Others were willing to conjecture that it was something new.

In 1507 cartographer Martin Waldseemüller created a revolutionary map. It placed a new continent in the ocean between western Europe and Cipangu (Japan), with Columbus's land of Paria at the top flowing into the coastline encountered by Portugal's Diego Álvares Cabral and explored by Vespucci. Waldseemüller called it "America" in honor of Amerigo Vespucci. It was the first time the word had been applied to the new lands.

Cartographer Martin Waldseemüller's 1507 map based on the voyages of Columbus and Vespucci was the first to use the term America *to describe the New World.*

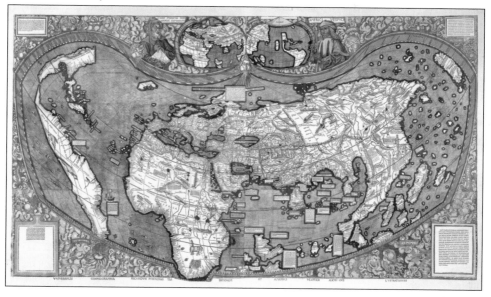

after several weeks at sea. There were talks of mutiny and of forcing Columbus to turn around and return to Spain. On October 9 he promised that they would do so if land was not sighted in the next three days. At 2:00 A.M. on October 12, a lookout on the *Pinta*, Rodrigo de Triana, sighted a white cliff shining in the moonlight and cried out, "Tierra! Tierra!"[20] (meaning "Land! Land!"). The following morning Columbus and his captains went ashore. They named the island San Salvador, Spanish for "Holy Savior." Today most historians believe that Columbus arrived at one of the islands of the Bahamas group, although the exact island on which he landed remains a subject for debate. As far as Columbus was concerned, however, he had reached the Indies.

Admiral of the Ocean Sea

Columbus's men stayed in these new waters until the following January. He was convinced that each island in the Bahamas was part of Cipangu, although the native people they encountered were nothing like the Japanese he expected. There were no large cities with gilded palaces, although some of the people did have gold jewelry. The inhabitants of these islands told Columbus that the gold came from lands farther south. On October 28 Columbus and his men explored the long coast of an area the inhabitants called Colba. Columbus believed he was on a peninsula of the Chinese mainland, but in fact, he had reached Cuba. He and his men also explored a nearby island they called Hispaniola. The *Santa Maria*

ran aground on its shores in December and had to be abandoned. Columbus took this as a divine indication that he should create a settlement there, and the local leader agreed to help. Since these native people had much more gold than any others Columbus had encountered, he had no shortage of volunteers from his crew to establish the colony.

In January 1493 the *Niña* and the *Pinta* set sail for home. While on board ship, Columbus composed an official report in the form of a long letter to Ferdinand and Isabella, touting his discoveries and promising that if they granted him another voyage, he would return to Spain with gold, cinnamon, rhubarb, slaves, and countless other valuable commodities. Columbus and his men encountered several storms and did not reach Spain until March. In April Columbus received a letter from Ferdinand and Isabella in which they used the titles they had promised: "Admiral of the Ocean Sea" and "Viceroy and Governor" of the lands he had discovered in the Indies. They congratulated him, invited him to visit them, and assured him that they would begin preparations for a second voyage immediately.

Later Voyages

News of Columbus's discoveries spread quickly across Europe. Before the end of April, his letter to Ferdinand and Isabella appeared in print, with a title that referred to "the Islands newly discovered in the Indian Ocean."[21] The letter was widely distributed across the continent but brought Columbus no great

European Voyages of Exploration, 1492–1533

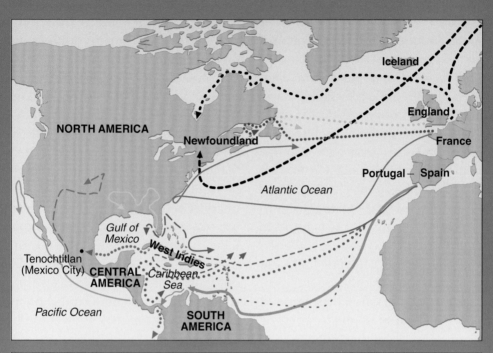

- - - -	Balboa 1510–1512	··········	Cortes 1519–1521
··········	Cabot 1497	————	De Soto 1539–1542
————	Cabrillo 1542–1543	- - - -	Hudson 1609
··········	Cartier 1534	···· ····	Hudson 1610
————	Columbus 1492	··········	Pizarro 1530–1533
- - - -	Columbus 1493	– – – –	Ponce de Leon 1513
· · · · ·	Columbus 1498	————	Verrazzano 1524
·········	Columbus 1502	————	Vespucci 1499
– – – –	Coronado 1540–1542		

Taken from: faculty.umf.maine.edu/waltersargent/public.www.web103/outline2umf103.06.htm.

fame. In fact, some observers wondered whether he had not arrived at another island chain in the Atlantic Ocean, like the Canary Islands, with no connection to the Indies whatsoever.

These opinions did not matter to Columbus. He was convinced he had reached the Indies. Over the next several years, with the king and queen financing his efforts, Columbus made three more voyages and encountered new lands. During this time, according to historian J.M. Roberts, "the historic name 'New World' was first applied to what had been found in the western hemisphere."[22] On his third expedition to the New World, Columbus and his men explored along a coast they called Paria and found an immense gulf into which four large rivers emptied. They were at the mouth of South America's Orinoco River, in today's Venezuela. On August 13, 1498, Columbus wrote, "I have come to believe that [the land beyond the gulf] is a mighty continent that was hitherto unknown."[23] Four days later, however, he changed his mind, believing that what he had found was actually the shores of the Garden of Eden. His Christian faith and all the geographical philosophers he had read taught him that Eden was to be found in the easternmost part of the world, near the equator, with a pleasant and agreeable climate. One writer had even said that Eden had a large lake from which the four rivers of Paradise flowed. He felt all the signs pointed to his conclusion.

Columbus's fourth and final voyage began in 1502. He explored the coastline of Central America as far south as Panama in search of a legendary passage to the Indian Ocean. He failed to find it, but he did find more gold and evidence of civilizations far more advanced than those he had encountered over the last decade. After two years he returned to Spain. Spanish efforts so far had not resulted in a route to the markets that the Portuguese had reached, although the native inhabitants in these new lands Columbus had encountered did appear to have significant amounts of gold. But this did not seem to justify the effort and the expense of further expeditions under his command.

Columbus died in 1506, convinced to the end that he had reached the Indies. In a way he had, because to this day the islands that he explored are collectively known as the West Indies. Regardless of his geographical shortcomings and his unwillingness to accept new ideas into his religion-based worldview, Columbus was an excellent navigator and mariner. He had not opened a new route to the riches of the Indian and Asian East, but those who followed in his wake discovered that these new lands had more surprises in store than they could have imagined.

Ponce de León and La Florida

Within five years of Columbus's death, Spanish colonies were growing on Hispaniola, Puerto Rico, and Cuba, supplied by regular fleets of ships from Europe. Some of the colonists had excellent relations with the native islanders, but others were more interested in the treasures that existed or that were rumored to exist throughout the area.

One Spaniard living on Puerto Rico named Juan Ponce de León wanted to investigate these rumors. In 1513 he sailed north with a fleet of three ships. He and his crew explored through the Bahamas and on April 2, 1513, they reached an unknown coast, which they

Treaty of Tordesillas

Shortly after Columbus's first voyage, Pope Alexander VI created a dividing line running from the North Pole to the South Pole "one hundred leagues [300 miles or 483km] towards the west . . . from any of the islands commonly known as the Azores and Cape Verdes." Any lands west of that line not already claimed by a Christian monarch would belong to Spain.

King John II of Portugal objected. He said that because the new lands were close to Portugal's Azores, they should be Portuguese territory. After months of negotiations, Portugal and Spain signed the Treaty of Tordesillas on June 7, 1494. The treaty declared a line similar to the pope's but at a distance of 370 leagues (about 1,110 miles or 1,786km) west of the Azores. To the east of the line was Portuguese dominion; to the west, Spanish.

In 1500 Portugal's Pedro Álvares Cabral accidently ventured too far west to sail around Africa and made landfall on an unknown coast. He believed it was east of the treaty line and informed the king. The territory became Portuguese and today is the Portuguese-speaking nation of Brazil.

Quoted in Daniel Boorstin. *The Discoverers.* New York: Random House, 1983, p. 248.

thought was another island. Because it was the Easter season, they named the land La Florida, after *Pascua Florida*, or "Festival of Flowers," the Spanish term for Easter. Ponce de León's exact landfall is uncertain, but he and his crew traveled along both the east and west coasts of the Florida Peninsula. They explored Florida's southwest coast, reversed course, and visited the Dry Tortugas and the Florida Keys before returning to Puerto Rico after almost eight months away.

Today Ponce de León's name is invariably associated with the search for the mythical Fountain of Youth. Historians, however, believe that this was not his motivation. As Morison points out, "At the age of thirty-nine, he could hardly have needed this cure himself."[24] Although he failed to find gold on the new shores he explored, he was not the only Spanish adventurer to reach previously unknown shores. Later that same year Vasco Núñez de Balboa became the first European to encounter the Pacific Ocean.

Balboa and the Mar del Sur

Balboa first arrived in the Caribbean in 1501 on a voyage that explored the Gulf of Darien, which lies between modern-day Panama and Colombia. After several years on Hispaniola, he returned to the Gulf of Darien region in 1509 and helped

On September 25, 1513, Vasco Núñez de Balboa became the first European to encounter the Pacific Ocean and claimed it for the king and queen of Spain.

establish the settlement of Santa Maria de l'Antigua del Darien in modern-day Panama. There he demonstrated an ability to foster excellent relations with the local inhabitants; he even married the daughter of a local chief. He also heard tales of a region "flowing with gold" as well as an area across a neighboring mountain range where one would "see another sea."[25] Balboa was determined to find both.

On September 1, 1513, he started inland. On a modern map this part of the Isthmus of Panama is only about 45 miles (72km) wide, and the mountains are no more than 1,000 feet (300m) tall. But the expedition, which included almost two hundred Spaniards and several hundred native guides and porters, encountered thick tropical forests with innumerable lakes and rivers. Wading or swimming across them took hours on end and went on day after day. Finally, on September 25 Balboa stood atop a ridge and sighted a body of water to the west shining in the sun. He called it the Mar del Sur, or "Southern Ocean," and reached its shores four days later. Wading into the surf, he declared that he was taking possession of it for the king and queen of Spain. Today it is called the Pacific Ocean.

Balboa crossed the isthmus several times over the coming years. Although he had accumulated a significant treasure in gold and pearls during his first crossing, he planned to build several ships on the western coast and sail south to the region rumored to be flowing with gold. However, he was arrested by a political rival in Santa Maria de l'Antigua del Darien on accusations that he was disloyal to Spain. He was executed in January 1519; it was just one action in a long series of power struggles among rival factions of the Spanish conquistadores.

Conquistadores

Some of the Spaniards in the New World were like Balboa. They were interested in the land and the native peoples who lived there, and they tried to establish good relations with them. Others were more ruthless, interested only in whatever riches they could accumulate, whether it was in gold, gems, pearls, or slaves. Both groups were called "conquistadores," Spanish for "conquerors." Today the term is often associated with accounts of brutality toward native peoples. Oral histories from those who were conquered and written firsthand accounts from Europeans contribute to modern knowledge of their actions.

One of the most important observers was Las Casas. He was a sixteenth-century chronicler and an astute observer of the actions of his countrymen. Before becoming a Catholic missionary, he was a conquistador in the early 1500s, and he witnessed fellow Spaniards enslaving and executing native people on Cuba and Hispaniola. For example, he described an incident in which native inhabitants greeted the newcomers "with [food], and delicate cheer . . . and they presented us with a great quantity of fish, and of bread, and other meat, together with all that they could do for us to the uttermost." The Spanish repaid this hospitality by "put[ting] them all to the edge of the sword in my presence, without any cause whatsoever, more than three thousand souls, which were set before us, men, women, and children."[26]

Las Casas spent the remainder of his life lobbying for better treatment of the native populations under Spanish dominion. He believed that, even if these individuals were not Christians, they still had souls and deserved to be treated humanely. His efforts succeeded when Spain passed a series of laws in 1542 designed to protect the native peoples, although many officials ignored the laws for their own personal benefit, resulting in continued mistreatment of the American Indians of the Spanish territories.

Another important account of the conquistador era comes from Bernal Díaz del Castillo. In his later years he published a memoir called "The True History of the Conquest of New Spain" that was based on his own observations and on interviews with his fellow soldiers. The book recounts his participation in over one hundred battles with native peoples as well as astute descriptions of the people and places he encountered. Today his narrative is recognized as a valuable record of the Spanish conquest of Mexico.

The Conquest of Mexico

By the end of the first decade of the 1500s, the Spanish had explored much of the coastline of present-day Central America. When they arrived on the Yucatán Peninsula in 1517, they saw evidence of rich native civilizations. Díaz del Castillo wrote of finding large buildings of stone with inlays of gold and gems and fanciful carvings of fish and birds. In April 1519 Hernán Cortés led an expedition from Cuba to the Yucatán coast and discovered that the local population had been subjugated recently by a powerful group called the Aztec, whose capital was high in the inland mountains. Cortés recruited many of the coastal peoples

to join him as he moved west against the Aztec capital, called Tenochtitlán.

Cortés and his countrymen were astounded by Tenochtitlán. The city was built on a lake, with causeways and an aqueduct connecting it to the lakeshore. Huge buildings and temples dominated the town, rivaling those the Spanish had left behind in Europe. The Aztec leader, Moctezuma II, knew the Spanish were coming, and he sent ambassadors to meet them during their march inland and as they reached Tenochtitlán on November 8. He invited them to stay in the capital, housing the troops in what Díaz del Castillo described as "a large building where there was room enough for us all. . . . There were separate beds for each of us. . . . The apartments and halls were very spacious, and those set apart for [Cortés] were furnished with carpets."[27] In the days and weeks that followed, Moctezuma allowed them to wander his capital, and Díaz del Castillo recorded visiting a huge market with all manner of products available, from gold, silver, and jewelry to everyday earthenware for cooking and storage.

Within two years, however, the wonders of Tenochtitlán were no more. The apparent mutual goodwill dissolved, and in the end Moctezuma was killed and the Spanish were victorious. Part of the lore of the conquistadores holds that Cortés conquered the Aztec capital with only five hundred men, fifteen horses, and six small cannons. This neglects the contributions of his native allies, who were more than willing to fight against their Aztec overlords. It also disregards the role that

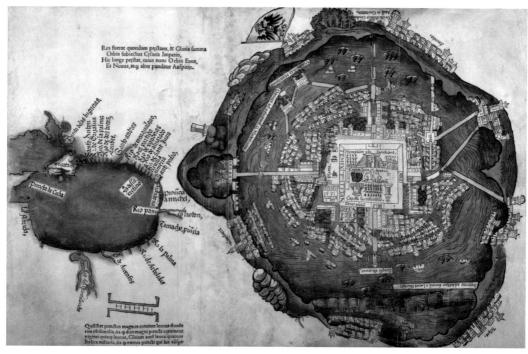

A Spanish chronicler's map of the Aztec city of Tenochtitlán. The Spaniards were astounded by the city, surprised that its causeways, aqueducts, temples, and huge buildings rivaled Europe's.

disease played in the conquest. The Aztec capital fell after a three-month siege in 1521 due to a combination of factors: a force with superior numbers and modern Spanish weaponry, and a plague of small-pox, a European disease against which the native population had no immunity. The conquistadores and their allies were ruthless in victory, killing thousands.

With the Aztec Empire in ruins, Cortés and other conquistadores spread out across Central America. For example, Pedro de Alvarado, who had been with Cortés during the final subjugation and massacre at Tenochtitlán, moved southeast into the highlands of the modern-day nations of Guatemala and El Salvador. He followed Cortés's example by

pitting native groups against each other to further his cause, and by 1530 much of the indigenous population had been conquered through mass executions and superior firepower. A decade later, as governor of Honduras, Alvarado was still looking for new lands to conquer, but he set his sights across the sea. He intended to sail from Mexico to China and outfitted an expedition of thirteen ships and over five hundred soldiers. However, he was fatally injured in an accident with a horse in July 1541, and his plans died with him. By that time other conquistadores had explored farther south into vast new territories and encountered additional native empires. One of these conquistadores was Francisco Pizarro.

La Malinche

One of the important players in the Spanish conquest of the Aztec capital of Tenochtitlán was a young Mexican woman who became part of Hernán Cortés's inner circle. Her original name was Malinal, but she is remembered today by two other names: Doña Marina and La Malinche.

She was a native Nahua who was sold into slavery after her father, a local chief, died and her mother remarried. She was one of twenty slaves presented as a gift to Cortés by the local Maya after he defeated them in 1519. When she was baptized, she chose the name Marina, and the Spanish added the honorific *Doña* ("Lady") to reflect her noble background. *Malinche* may be the Spanish version of "Malin" plus the Nahuatl honorific *tzin*.

The conquistadores discovered that she spoke both Maya and her native Nahuatl, which was the common language of central Mexico at the time. She translated Nahuatl into Maya; a Spaniard with Cortés who understood Maya then translated into Spanish for Cortés. Once she learned Spanish, she translated for Cortés directly. She served a vital role in communicating with Moctezuma II and other Aztec officials; pictorial versions of the events show her always at Cortés's side.

"I Will Be No Man's Tributary"

Francisco Pizarro first came to the Spanish settlements in 1510 and joined Balboa in his first expedition to the Pacific Ocean in 1513. Like Balboa and others, he had heard native stories of rich countries to the south. In 1524 and 1526 he and two partners outfitted expeditions that sailed along the Pacific coastline, reaching below the equator. There they visited several towns along the coastline, including Tumbes, near the modern-day border of Ecuador and Peru. These towns had lavish temples, buildings made of stone, fertile fields for cultivation, and aqueducts to bring water from the coastal mountains. At each stop Pizarro and his partners heard about a rich inland empire ruled by native people called the Inca; the tales seemed to confirm the stories they had heard in Panama. But when they returned to Panama, the governor refused to help pay for further explorations. Pizarro journeyed back to Spain to try to receive royal permission for the venture.

The Spanish king, Charles V, was fascinated by Pizarro's stories. Pizarro showed the king several native inhabitants of the area; the human prisoners were not nearly as interesting to the king as the captive llama, which was unknown to Europeans at the time. In 1529 the king granted Pizarro permission to explore and claim the territory for Spain. In 1532 Pizarro marched inland from Tumbes and established a settlement called San Miguel de Piura in July. There he received an envoy from Atahualpa, the leader of the Inca, who invited the Spanish to meet him at a mountain retreat called Cajamarca.

It took Pizarro nearly two months to reach Cajamarca. He brought with him 180 men and twenty-seven horses. Atahualpa met the conquistador in the town square. While the square filled with Atahualpa's men, the Spanish surrounded them with their firearms concealed. Atahualpa refused to acknowledge that Charles was now his king; according to one account, he said, "I will be no man's tributary."[28] When he also refused to acknowledge the Catholic Church's authority, Pizarro ordered his men to open fire and then charge with his cavalry. According to historian Chris Harman, "There was nowhere for the Incas to flee. According to Spanish estimates, 2,000 Incas died, according to Inca estimates 10,000."[29] Atahualpa was captured and unsuccessfully tried to buy his freedom with enough gold to fill a

Francisco Pizarro led the conquest of the Inca Empire in Peru. This illustration depicts the meeting of Pizarro with Inca leader Atahualpa in Cajamarca.

room measuring 22 feet by 17 feet (6.7m by 5.2m) and with enough silver to fill a smaller room twice. Pizarro put him on trial for plotting against the Spanish, and he was executed on July 26, 1533.

When Pizarro invaded and captured the Incan capital of Cuzco that same year, the collapse of the Incan Empire was complete. Pizarro established his own capital in 1535 at Lima, along the coastline, where he lived until he was assassinated in 1541 by supporters of a political rival. He left behind a legacy of conquest against heavy odds, but also one of death and destruction, because thousands of native people died from starvation, European diseases, and forced labor in Peruvian silver mines. According to Harman, "The indigenous population of the empire fell by between a half and three-quarters."[30] One Spanish official noted, "The entire country was calm and well-nourished [in Incan times], whereas today we see only infinite deserted villages on all the roads in the kingdom."[31]

Pedro de Valdivia

From their base in Peru, the Spanish began to explore farther south into South America. In 1536 Diego de Almagro left Cuzco and, with the assistance of native guides, made an arduous crossing of the Andes mountain range at elevations of more than 12,000 feet (3,658m), and traveled south into modern-day Chile. Almagro and his men antagonized the indigenous populations, especially when they discovered there was no vast treasure to plunder, and eventually returned to Peru in 1537 via the coastal Atacama Desert.

A few years later Pedro de Valdivia, one of Pizarro's officers, received permission to lead an expedition back into Chile. Valdivia had a difficult time recruiting men because of the tales told by those who had been with Almagro. Nonetheless, he left Cuzco in January 1540 with almost one thousand redundant Indians to carry equipment and supplies, plus swine, horses, and seeds for planting. He avoided the mountains by crossing the desert, which was and remains one of the driest environments on the planet. After five grueling months, they reached the fertile Copiapó River valley. The local people they met during the trek were unhappy to see the Spanish return, but Valdivia was able to improve relations through promises of fair treatment and gifts to native leaders.

Traveling farther south, Valdivia's expedition reached the Mapocho River valley in December, and after negotiations with the local chieftains, Valdivia formally founded a town he called Santiago de la Nueva Extremedura, after Saint James (*Santiago*) and his native region in Spain (*Extremedura*). Today better known as simply Santiago, it is the capital of modern-day Chile.

The initially positive relations with the local populations soured as the Spanish continued along the coastline, especially as they began to force the inhabitants to work in several gold mines. In September 1541 the local inhabitants attacked Santiago while Valdivia, now the royal governor of the province, was dealing with another uprising. A small garrison held out until Valdivia returned. The town was burned to the ground, and the settlers were left with few provisions but decided to stay. Reinforcements from Peru aided the reconstruction of the town, and by 1544 Valdivia was able to send new expeditions along the coastline. One made landings at the sites of what became the cities of Concepción and Valdivia (which was named in the conquistador's honor).

The End of a Conquistador

Further expansion by the Spanish encountered increasingly hostile resistance from the native populations. Valdivia and a group of soldiers were killed in December 1553 during a native uprising, and no definitive accounts of his death exist. Valdivia's exploits in Chile survive in part due to twelve letters he wrote to Charles in which he documented his successes and setbacks.

As a whole, Valdivia's life typified the career of many conquistadores. He achieved fame and honors in association with the exploits of another adventurer, and then struck out on his own. By the time of his death, the era of the conquistador was passing. The wealthiest native empires had been sacked and looted, with the treasures flowing back to Europe. The Age of Exploration, however, was far from over. Two sixteenth-century ocean voyages demonstrated that there were farther horizons yet to explore.

Chapter Three

Around the World

During the early sixteenth century, Spain and Portugal established control of vital trade routes on the world's oceans. Portugal had a virtual monopoly on trade in the Indian Ocean and the South China Sea. Spain sent large flotillas to the New World with supplies for growing colonies, and these ships returned laden with treasures from native empires.

With Portugal in the east and Spain in the west, there remained a great unknown for cartographers, geographers, and rulers alike. No one was completely sure where east and west met and what new lands were yet to be discovered. There was also the matter of 1494's Treaty of Tordesillas and its line of demarcation. No one knew how the Indies would be divided if the line were extended around the world. A native of Portugal sailing for Spain helped answer the question.

Ferdinand Magellan

Ferdinand Magellan was born around 1480 in northern Portugal, and by age twenty-five he was sailing to ports in the Indian Ocean. He then served with Afonso de Albuquerque during the exploration of the Spice Islands (today's Moluccas) in modern-day Indonesia and the conquest of Malacca in modern-day Malaysia. When he returned to Portugal in 1512, he had risen to the rank of captain. Over the next several years, he was accused of financial mismanagement by his superior officers and by King Manuel I. The final straw for Magellan came in 1517 when Manuel humiliated him by refusing his offer of allegiance in front of the king's inner circle. Magellan renounced his Portuguese loyalty and left for Spain.

Once in Spain Magellan reconnected with some of his friends from his adventures in Asia and made new ones among the elite of Spanish society. He also learned of new explorations in the New World, including voyages along the east coast of South America. During an audience with the Spanish king Charles V, he shared a premise and made a specific proposal. He began with the line of demarcation, which had been established by the 1494 Treaty of Tordesillas between Portugal and Spain. The imaginary line ran north to south in the Atlantic Ocean, dividing Spanish domains to the west from Portuguese domains to the east. Magellan's premise was that if the line were extended to the far side of the

Ferdinand Magellan led the first expedition to circumnavigate the globe in 1519.

world, the Moluccas would fall into the Spanish hemisphere, and he was willing to prove it. His proposal, according to Daniel J.Boorstin, "was to reach the Spice Islands by sailing westward. [His] plan was . . . precise —to find a strait at the extreme tip of South America."[32]

Charles approved the plan and provided essential royal backing during the next eighteen months while Magellan and his partners gathered resources, recruited sailors, and outfitted five ships. Portuguese spies tried their best to keep the fleet from sailing in order to keep the Spanish out of the Indies. Historian V.R. LaLonde points out that Magellan had other challenges as well:

> Magellan also had to contend with Spanish financiers anxious to [restrict] trade so as to keep market prices high. These financiers used their influence to place men of their choosing into key positions in the fleet. The council of financiers chose three out of five captains, four out of five pilots, and half of the first lieutenants, master-at-arms, and stewards. The fleet's second-in-command, Juan de Cartagena, was also chosen by the council and known as a troublemaker who was plotting mutiny before the fleet was out of sight of land.[33]

Magellan's fleet, called the Armada de Molucca, consisted of five ships: the *Trinidad* (under Magellan's command), *San Antonio* (the largest of the fleet), *Concepción*, *Santiago*, and *Victoria*. The ships left Seville, Spain, on August 10, 1519; after final preparations on the coast of Spain, the fleet set sail into the Atlantic on September 20.

Across the Atlantic

The 270 men of Magellan's fleet came from diverse backgrounds. There were about forty Portuguese, including Magellan's brother-in-law, along with Italians, French, Germans, Greeks, and one Englishman, as well as Spaniards. One of the Italians was an adventurer named Antonio Pigafetta, who had volunteered to be Magellan's assistant and to keep an official account of the voyage. Additionally, a young man named Enrique, who had been by Magellan's side since his days in the East, was on board, but Magellan's longtime friend from Portugal, Rui Faleiro, decided not to go along because his astrologer predicted he would not survive the trip.

Almost from the beginning, Juan de Cartagena, commanding *San Antonio*, and his Spanish colleagues—Captains Quesada of the *Concepción* and Mendoza of the *Victoria*—began to question Magellan's decisions. After stopping in the Canary Islands and the Azores, Magellan sailed along the African coast; Cartagena argued that they should sail straight out to sea. Their disputes became so intense that at one point during the crossing, Magellan stripped Cartagena of his command and imprisoned him on board before reassigning him to a lower rank.

After two months at sea, the fleet reached the coast of Brazil. The ships

Enrique of Malaya

During Ferdinand Magellan's service to Portugal, he traveled to the Moluccas and participated in the capture of Malacca in 1511. Historians believe that it was then that he first encountered a young man who became his slave and companion for the rest of his life. This young man, whose original name is unknown, was a native of the Malay Peninsula and was baptized as Enrique.

Enrique shared the hardships and triumphs of Magellan's voyage through the strait that bears his master's name and across the Pacific. He proved instrumental in fostering friendly relations between the explorers and the islanders in the Philippines, as he and they spoke a common dialect.

After Magellan's death, Enrique refused to cooperate with the other officers. He had been freed by Magellan in his will, and he felt no loyalty to any of the others. Some historians theorize that the attack on Magellan's officers and men that occurred on Cebu on May 1, 1521, was due to rumors spread by Enrique. Regardless of his role in the events, he disappears from the historical record at that point and was likely left behind when the expedition left the island.

sailed south to avoid Portuguese territory and anchored in the harbor of present-day Rio de Janeiro on December 13, 1519. There they enjoyed two weeks of pleasant Southern Hemisphere late spring weather. They made repairs and traded with the native people, who were more than willing to exchange fresh supplies of food and water for what the Europeans felt were insignificant items. For example, the native inhabitants, who had no access to iron, found metal objects particularly valuable. According to Pigafetta, "The people of this place gave for a knife or a fishhook five or six fowls, and for a comb a [pair] of geese. For a small mirror or a pair of scissors, they gave as many fish as ten men could have eaten. . . . And for a king of playing cards . . . they gave me five fowls, and even thought they cheated me."[34] After celebrating Christmas Day in the harbor, the explorers continued south on December 26 in search of a passage to the Pacific.

Port San Julián

By February 1520 the Armada de Molucca had reached the Río de la Plata estuary along the South American coast, between modern-day Uruguay and Argentina. The best information of the day surmised that a strait to the Pacific was located there; earlier adventurers had written about finding a broad opening in the land at this approximate latitude but had been unable to go farther. Magellan sent the *Santiago*, the smallest ship, into the estuary in hopes of finding it led farther west. Captain Serrano returned with the disappointing news that the bay was fed by two freshwater rivers.

Magellan was convinced that the fabled strait could not be much farther south. He hoped to find it before the Southern Hemisphere autumn arrived in April. A series of storms then intervened. According to Samuel Eliot Morison, "For three weeks, they made only about 120 miles southwesterly, and no sun appeared."[35] Unrelenting winds

shredded their sails and threatened to drive them ashore; towering waves toppled masts and tore away rigging. Finally, on March 31 Magellan entered a bay he called Port San Julián and decided to wait out the winter. The very next day, however, Magellan faced a huge challenge that could decide the fate of the entire expedition. On that Easter Sunday, April 1, 1520, the captains of the *Concepcíon*, *San Antonio*, and *Victoria* mutinied, demanding he abandon his quest and return to Spain.

Facing this challenge to his command, Magellan sent loyal men from the *Trini-*

Magellan's five ships encountered treacherous storms for several weeks in early 1520 along the South American coast before finding a safe harbor.

dad to the *Victoria* with orders to kill the ship's captain if he refused to rejoin Magellan. Mendoza laughed at the proposal and was quickly executed. The rest of the crew surrendered to Magellan's men. Magellan then positioned the *Victoria*, *Trinidad*, and *Santiago* across the mouth of the harbor. The mutineers realized they were now outnumbered and surrendered by day's end. Quesada of the *Concepción* was deemed the ringleader and was executed. His and Mendoza's bodies were placed on gallows on the shore as a reminder of their actions. In addition, Cartagena and a priest were found guilty of conspiring with the mutineers and were sentenced to be marooned when the expedition left Port San Julián.

The remainder of the autumn and winter in Port San Julián passed without further talk of mutiny. Magellan kept the men busy scouring the countryside for food, fishing, and cleaning and repairing the vessels. The *Santiago* ran aground in May and could not be salvaged. In August Magellan carried out the sentence against Cartagena and the priest by marooning them on an island in the harbor. The remaining four ships of the Armada de Molucca left Port San Julián and continued their southward journey.

Frustration and Elation

Storms continued to impede their progress until October, when favorable northerly winds arose to speed them southward. On October 21 they noticed an elongated cape extending into open waters and a wide opening into the land.

Vasquito Gallego, an apprentice seaman on board the *Victoria*, later recalled the gradual realization that they might have found something significant. As they sailed into the opening, according to Gallego, "they thought it was a river. . . . Continuing that way, they found deep salt water and strong currents, appearing to be a strait and the mouth of a big gulf that might be discharging into it."[36] They had indeed reached the fabled strait. Antonio Pigafetta attributed the discovery to a divine intercession, writing, "On the Festival of the Eleven Thousand Virgins, we found by a miracle a strait which we called the Cape of the Eleven Thousand Virgins."[37] The landmark entrance to the strait retains a form of that name today: Cabo Vírgenes, or Cape Virgins.

The strait was unlike anything any of the men had ever seen. Instead of a short passage from one body of water to the next, such as the Strait of Gibraltar, the ships had to navigate a maze of islands and fjords, with towering glaciers and abundant bird and marine life. By November 1, All Saints Day, they were convinced that they were indeed navigating a strait and declared it Estrecho de Todos los Santos, or "All Saints Strait." Soon afterward, however, the *San Antonio* disappeared while separated from the other ships. The *San Antonio*'s disgruntled pilot and his allies had mutinied, put the captain in chains, and sailed for Spain, taking with them a significant amount of the fleet's food supplies.

After searching for the *San Antonio* for several days, Magellan realized the ship had deserted the expedition. The three remaining ships sailed on. The passage, which had been leading them west-southwest, abruptly turned north-north-west. On November 28 they reached the Pacific Ocean, taking thirty-eight days to navigate a tortuous 334-mile (538km) passage that is now called the Strait of Magellan in his honor.

Three Months Without Fresh Food

Upon exiting the strait, Magellan and the men (now numbering about two hundred) were overjoyed and felt that they were well prepared for the remainder of their quest. At every opportunity while in the strait, they had filled their water barrels from glacier-fed waterfalls, caught fish, and gathered wild celery and other plants that modern science identifies as rich in vitamin C. It is important to remember that this western ocean had been sighted by Balboa only seven years earlier, and no Europeans had spent any time on its open waters. Most estimates of the ocean's size harked back to Ptolemy; Magellan and his contemporaries believed that a short passage awaited them before they reached the Spice Islands. According to Morison, "All estimates in Magellan's hands, whether literary or cartographical, were at least 80 per cent short of the truth."[38]

The ships steered north and northwest along the coast of modern-day Chile before Magellan turned west. Favorable winds blew across their sterns, and the land quickly dropped below the horizon. The familiar routines at sea returned, and with them, the familiar challenges of long ocean voyages. But the ocean was far larger than expected. Pigafetta recorded that the men went "three months and twenty days without getting any kind of fresh food."[39] They dealt with rancid water, putrid meat, and the eventual onset of scurvy. Being ill did not excuse sailors from working on deck, hoisting the sails, and standing watch. During that period thirty men died. The only saving grace was that they had excellent weather the entire time.

They crossed the equator on February 13, 1521, and finally sighted land on March 6. They had reached Guam in the Mariana Islands, which are about 1,000 miles (1,609km) west of the Hawaiian Islands. They tarried for three days, getting fresh water and food from the native islanders, before heading back into the open ocean. Refreshed and in better health, they sailed west-southwest, and just a week later they reached the group of islands now called the Philippines. On March 28 a small boat arrived from the nearby island called Limasawa. Magellan's Malaysian companion, Enrique, hailed them in his native language, and they replied in kind. As Morison puts it, "West had met East at last by circling the globe. Enrique may have been the first to do it."[40]

Death in the Philippines

The Europeans, however, were not the first strangers to reach these shores. As they spoke with the islanders of Limasawa and nearby Cebu, they heard tales of other ships that came from afar to trade with the islanders. The Limasawans produced Chinese products such as porcelain and silk as proof. When Magellan arrived at Cebu, he discovered that a ship from Thailand had recently departed, leaving one of their traders with the islanders. The Europeans were impressed by this society, especially when compared with the ones they had encountered elsewhere on their odyssey.

Shortly thereafter, Sula, one of the leaders of the neighboring island of Mactan, sent one of his sons to visit Magellan. Sula and the king of Cebu were allies, and through his son, he asked Magellan to join him in an attack against his enemy on Mactan. Magellan agreed,

much to the consternation of his officers. Pigafetta wrote, "We begged him repeatedly not to go, but, he . . . refused"[41] to change his mind.

The expedition to Mactan on April 27, 1521, was a disaster. The island defenders had adequate time to prepare for the attack, understood the terrain on which they were fighting, had superior numbers, and took advantage of the Spaniards' weaknesses. They aimed their spears and poisoned arrows for the invaders' legs, which were unprotected by their armor. Magellan was wounded repeatedly by their arrows, spears, and swords with long, curved blades. He fell dead facedown on the beach, trying to protect his retreating men. His body was never recovered.

Magellan was killed after he and his men invaded the island of Mactan in the Philippines in 1521.

To the Spice Islands

Following Magellan's death, the remaining officers decided they should continue to the Spice Islands as planned. The king of Cebu, however, feared retribution from Mactan once the armada left and, believing a rumor that the Europeans planned to kidnap him, invited the ships' leaders to a grand banquet. Thirty men accepted, and all but two were killed by the islanders.

The survivors set sail as quickly as possible. There were now 115 men remaining of the 260 who had left Spain. Because they felt that they were now too few in number to man all three ships, they burned the *Concepción* and consolidated their crews and supplies into the *Trinidad* and the *Victoria*. They elected new officers; João Lopes Carvalho, the former pilot of the *Concepción*, became the armada's new leader; and Juan Sebastián Elcano, the *Concepción*'s former captain, took over command of the *Victoria*. Without Magellan's powerful presence, however, his successors demonstrated their true character. For example, during a visit to Borneo, Carvalho kidnapped three women and kept them on board the *Trinidad* as his slaves. His men objected, and he was forced to pay a large ransom to his own men in order to stay alive. It marked the start of a descent into piracy.

They spent the summer and early fall capturing ships and arguing among

The Treaty of Zaragoza

When Magellan reached the Philippines in 1521, they were unknown to European cartographers. The islands also posed a vexing problem for Spanish and Portuguese politicians. The Portuguese claimed that the Spice Islands were in their half of the world as defined by the 1494 Treaty of Tordesillas. But no one knew with certainty where the treaty's line of demarcation would exist on the far side of the world or where the Spice Islands and the Philippines were located in relation to the line.

Spain and Portugal met several times during the 1520s to determine the Treaty of Tordesillas's antemeridian, or the location of the treaty's line on the exact opposite side of the globe. In 1529 the two nations agreed in the Treaty of Zaragoza that the antemeridian placed the Spice Islands and Magellan's Philippines within the Portuguese hemisphere. Spain relinquished all claim to both island groups.

In 1565, however, the Spanish returned to the Philippines and established a trading post at Manila. The Portuguese protested but did not press their claim, in part due to the lack of valuable spices found there.

themselves. After one dispute, Carvalho was stripped of his command in favor of Gonzalo Goméz de Espinosa. The *Trinidad* and the *Victoria* eventually found their way to the Moluccas in November 1521, and having reached their goal, relations improved among the men. They spent several weeks there, purchasing cloves, cinnamon, nutmeg, and mace and filling the holds of the remaining ships.

The officers wanted to ensure that the precious cargoes returned to Spain. They decided that Espinosa and the *Trinidad* would recross the Pacific and head for Panama, where the cinnamon, nutmeg, and mace would be carried cross-country to the Caribbean and then shipped back to Europe. Elcano and the *Victoria* would sail west with the cargo of cloves through the Indian Ocean and around Africa.

Homeward Bound

The ambitious plan did not go as planned; although the *Victoria* set sail for home on December 21, repairs delayed the *Trinidad*'s departure until April 6, 1522. Espinosa barely made it as far east as the Mariana Islands before being blown back to the Philippines. Illnesses and disease claimed half his men. When the *Trinidad* returned to the Moluccas in the autumn, those aboard were imprisoned by the captain of a Portuguese fleet that had arrived in the interim to enforce Portugal's monopoly. Only four men survived to return to Spain.

The *Victoria*, on the other hand, did return to Spain. The crew members endured monstrous storms, including one that, according to Pigafetta, prevented them from rounding the Cape of Good Hope for nine weeks. They performed funerals at sea as scurvy claimed more victims. After crossing the equator for the fourth time on June 8, 1522, off the coast of West Africa, Pigafetta recorded that "we sailed northwest for two months continually without taking on any fresh food or water. . . . Twenty-one men died during that short time."[42]

Finally, on September 8, 1522, the *Victoria* and its skeleton crew limped into Seville's harbor. They had been gone just over three years. Eighteen out of sixty men who had left the Moluccas had survived the ordeal. They had covered 37,560 miles (60,447km), more than one and a half times the circumference of the earth.

Magellan's Legacy

Although Magellan did not live to return to Spain, the survivors had succeeded in reaching the East by sailing west. The legacy of the effort was the realization of the true size of the planet. Magellan's discovery of the vast distances between the Americas and Asia and the interconnected nature of the great oceans were at least as important as the discovery of the Strait of Magellan.

Spain was unable to take advantage of Magellan's pioneering route. Charles sponsored several attempts over the next few years, but each attempt ended in failure. Additionally, the king's political adventures in Europe bankrupted his nation. In 1529 Charles renounced all claims to the Moluccas in return for a loan from Portugal. It would be another fifty years before another mariner repeated Magellan's feat. He was neither Spanish nor Portuguese; he was English.

England and Spain

By the 1560s English ships were sailing the Atlantic Ocean in increasing numbers. Men such as John Hawkins commanded ships that visited West African ports to buy slaves to be sold in the West Indies. The Spanish banned all English ships from trading in their Caribbean ports, but Hawkins and others defied the ban. In 1568 Hawkins's fleet of six ships was attacked by Spanish ships at San Juan de Ulúa (near present-day Veracruz), Mexico, and suffered heavy losses. Four ships were destroyed and five hundred men were killed.

One of the survivors was Francis Drake, commander of the *Judith*. Drake was in his late twenties and on his second voyage to the New World. Like Hawkins and others who survived the battle, he believed that the Spanish fleet had violated a truce by attacking the English. The defeat, in the words of Morison, "seems to have given him an inextinguishable lust for revenge."[43] Drake eventually became one of England's most prominent mariners in his nation's undeclared war with Spain.

The conflict centered on not only the desire for profit but the Protestant Reformation that was raging in Europe. England had become a Protestant nation, but Spain remained staunchly Catholic. England's Queen Elizabeth I gave unspoken approval to efforts that would strengthen her nation and weaken Spain. She permitted Drake and others to capture Spanish treasure from the New World in return for a portion of the profits. These mariners were called privateers; they were not undertaking official government activities as part of the English navy, but they were acting in much the same manner. The Spanish called them pirates for what they felt was the theft of Spanish property. In their eyes Drake was one of the worst offenders.

Privateering and Preparations

Over the next several years, Drake commanded privateering voyages along the Spanish Main, the term given to the coastlines of the New World from Florida to Venezuela. For example, in 1572 he attacked towns along Panama's east coast, capturing the town of Nombre de Dios. He also led an overland expedition that took him within sight of the Pacific Ocean. He captured a substantial amount of treasure and returned to England in 1573.

Drake understood that this booty came from Spanish dominions in Peru. It was shipped north on vessels sailing the Pacific coastline and then brought overland across the Isthmus of Panama for shipment to Spain. Back in England, he proposed a voyage that would raid the treasure before it reached Panama. To do so, he would have to sail around the tip of South America. He and several partners formed a syndicate to finance and share in the profits from a venture, which apparently had the support

English captain Francis Drake was a privateer who preyed on Spanish treasure ships in the Caribbean. Later, he was the first Englishman to reach the Pacific Ocean and to circumnavigate the globe.

of Elizabeth. According to Drake, she told him, "So it is that I would gladly be revenged upon the King of Spain for [multiple defeats and insults] that I have received!"[44]

Drake assembled a fleet of five ships and about 160 men in Plymouth, England, in the summer of 1577. The pri-vateers sailed south from England on December 13 and captured several Spanish and Portuguese prizes along the West African coast. When they captured a Portuguese ship named the *Maria* in the Cape Verde Islands, they removed the cargo and put the crew ashore, adding the ship to their fleet. The *Maria*'s pilot,

The Discovery of Cape Horn

In the years following Drake's voyage around the world, other mariners accomplished the same feat. Each did so by sailing through the Strait of Magellan. Each considered that Tierra del Fuego, the land on the south side of the entrance to the strait, was a separate landmass. A pair of Dutchmen changed that perception.

In 1615 Willem Schouten and Jacob Le Maire led a pair of ships to see whether an alternative route existed to the Strait of Magellan. They left Netherlands in June 1615, and in January 1616, sailing far south of Magellan's Cape Virgins, they sighted an opening and sailed into it. On January 29 they passed a high point of land, covered with snow, that they named Cape Horn, for Schouten's hometown of Hoorn. By February 12 they calculated they were west of the Strait of Magellan. They crossed the Pacific and returned to Netherlands in July 1617.

Schouten and Le Maire's compatriots were not impressed by the feat, and Dutch merchants continued to favor the route around southern Africa to reach Asia. Consequently, Schouten and Le Maire's discoveries are little known outside the seafaring community.

Dutch explorers Willem Schouten and Jakob Le Maire are welcomed by the natives of Cape Horn Island.

Nuna da Silva, volunteered to guide the fleet in South American waters, and in February 1578 the fleet of six vessels headed across the Atlantic.

A Visit to Port San Julián

Drake's fleet reached the Brazilian coast in April and sailed south. Two ships in irreparable condition were abandoned and burned before they reached Port San Julián on June 20. This was the same harbor where Magellan had spent the southern winter of 1520. Magellan's voyage was well known among Drake's men, including the stories of the mutiny of April 1. In the harbor, according to Drake's chaplain, Francis Fletcher, "we found a gibbet [gallows] standing upon the [shore], which we supposed to be the place where *Magellan* did execution upon some of his disobedient and rebellious company."[45]

Winter was just starting in the Southern Hemisphere, but Drake was unwilling to spend much time in Port San Julián. He decided to risk passing through the Strait of Magellan in winter. He addressed his men and exhorted them to share equally in the tasks that lay ahead: "I must have the [officer] to haul and draw with the mariner and the mariner with the [officer]. What! let us show ourselves all to be of a company, and let us not give occasion to the enemy to rejoice at our decay and overthrow. I would know him that would refuse to set his hand to a rope, but know that there is not any such here."[46]

Before leaving Port San Julián, Drake's men stripped and burned a third ship,

leaving them with three to continue the voyage: the *Elizabeth*, the *Marygold*, and Drake's ship, the *Golden Hind*. The fleet set sail from Port San Julián on August 17, 1578, and entered the strait on August 21.

The Seas "Are But One!"

Drake's fleet took a mere sixteen days to reach the Pacific in the middle of a Southern Hemisphere winter. During the north-northwest leg of the passage, they anchored in several sheltered coves to collect wild berries and fresh herbs that helped relieve the sailors' scurvy. Once they entered the Pacific, however, their luck turned for the worse. Storms buffeted the ships for nearly a month. By October the fleet was down to one ship. The *Marygold* was last seen along the Chilean coast in a storm and was lost with twenty-eight men on board, and the *Elizabeth* deserted, sailing back through the strait without Drake's permission to return to England.

When the storms finally abated, Drake sighted an island now called Henderson Island. He believed he had been blown so far south that he had reached the most southerly point of the continent. He declared that beyond it, "there is no main[land] nor Island to be seen in the Southwards, but that the Atlantic Ocean and the South Sea [Pacific Ocean], meet in a most large and free scope. The [Atlantic] and the South Sea are but one!"[47]

Henderson Island is approximately 60 miles (100km) northwest of the actual tip of South America, but Drake had discovered that the territory at the end of the continent, now called Tierra del Fuego, was not connected to a great landmass at the bottom of the world, as centuries of maps by Ptolemy and others had depicted. Although historians agree that Drake did not actually sail farther south than Henderson Island and into the open ocean south of Cape Horn, the junction of the Pacific and Atlantic Oceans is called Drake Passage in his honor. From this region, Drake sailed north from Henderson Island, finding favorable winds along the coast of Chile.

Spanish Prizes

In the years since Magellan's voyage, Spanish territory had expanded south from Peru into modern-day Chile, although most of the settlements were small villages with few inhabitants. Drake and his men surprised a variety of unarmed and unsuspecting merchant ships that were not expecting to find an English ship where none had appeared before. They also landed at a variety of settlements, such as Valparaíso and Arica in Chile and Lima in Peru, overwhelming the few soldiers at hand and making off with treasures such as casks of wine, bars of silver, and gold coins. The men looted homes and churches but refrained from violence against the inhabitants.

Drake spoke enough Spanish that he was able to converse with his opponents and learn about other treasures that awaited him along the coast. For example, after sailing into Lima's port and plundering a dozen ships, he learned of a greater prize that had just left port. This was the *Nuestra Señora de la Concepción*, a treasure ship bound for Panama. The *Golden Hind* was a faster ship than the heavily laden *Nuestra Señora de la Concepción*, and Drake caught up with it two weeks later, on March 1, 1579. Drake came alongside the Spanish ship after nightfall and demanded its surrender. The Spanish captain had not expected an English ship in the Pacific and was caught by surprise. He refused to surrender; Drake opened fire with the *Golden Hind*'s cannons, which destroyed one of the *Nuestra Señora de la Concepción*'s masts. Drake sent an armed party of men aboard, and they overwhelmed the Spanish crew after a short struggle. It took Drake's men three days to unload the treasure from the Spanish ship before they sent it on its way with a letter of safe conduct, which guaranteed it safety from any other English ships.

After taking a variety of other prizes, including a ship with up-to-date charts and maps of the Pacific, Drake decided to head north, away from Spanish settlements. In so doing he explored and visited a coastline unseen by European eyes.

Nova Albion

During the spring of 1579, Drake sailed north beyond modern-day Mexico and traveled perhaps as far north as present-day Oregon before turning south again. The *Golden Hind* needed repairs, and the crew needed supplies before crossing the Pacific, so they sailed along the coast in search of a safe harbor. On June 17 they sailed into a protected cove and

Sir Francis Drake's galleon the Golden Hind *was the scourge of the Spanish Main.*

drove the ship gently ashore in a process called careening, which allows men to make repairs to areas normally below the waterline. The sailors also built an encampment on shore, which drew the attention of the local inhabitants.

No one knows for sure exactly where Drake landed. Most historians believe it was in a bay on the Point Reyes Peninsula in modern-day California, about 40 miles (64km) north of San Francisco. Today the landmark is called Drake's

Bay. If this is correct, then the men and women who came to see the strangers on their shore were Miwok, who lived along this coastline. They made long speeches that befuddled the English, and no doubt the reverse was true as the English tried to explain their own actions. When the man the English believed was the Miwok leader placed a headdress on Drake, the English took it as a sign that the locals were pledging allegiance to them and to Elizabeth. Consequently, Drake declared the land as English territory. According to Fletcher, Drake called the country "*Nova Albion*, and that for two causes: the one, in respect of the white banks and cliffs, which lie towards the sea: and the other, because it might have some [similarity] with our country in name,"[48] because Albion was an ancient name for Great Britain.

Five weeks passed before the repairs were made and provisions were laid in for the Pacific crossing. On July 23 the *Golden Hind* left the unknown Nova Albion astern. Drake's next destination was the Moluccas.

Homeward Bound

Drake's ship sailed west for a little more than two months before reaching land, probably one of the islands in the Palau group. Although he was now close to the Philippines, he bypassed them and sailed directly for the Moluccas. When he arrived at the Moluccan island of Ternate, the local ruler sent representatives to investigate Drake and his crew, and the ruler was pleased to discover

that they were neither Spanish nor Portuguese. He and Drake discussed the opportunity to break Portugal's monopoly on the spice trade, and Drake eventually purchased 6 tons (5.4t) of cloves. Drake and his men spent less than a week at Ternate before sailing away on November 6, 1579. They stopped at an uninhabited island they called Crab Island (for the abundant crabs found there) to careen and repair the *Golden Hind*, which took another month.

After departing Crab Island, the ship ran aground on a reef off the east coast of Celebes in modern-day Indonesia on January 8, 1580. For three days the crew tried to dislodge the ship, tossing cannons, sacks of flour and beans, and half of the cargo of cloves overboard—but none of the Spanish treasure—in an attempt to lighten the ship. Finally, the wind shifted and the ship eased off the reef without damage. They turned west and sailed along the southern coast of Java before crossing the Indian Ocean and rounding the Cape of Good Hope in June, following in the wake of Elcano's *Victoria* in 1522. Their supplies lasted until they reached the west coast of Africa; when they stopped at a river in modern-day Sierra Leone to take on supplies of wood and fresh water in July, it was their first stop since Java. They arrived in Plymouth, England, on September 26, 1580, having been away for two years and nine months.

Aftermath

Drake's voyage had demonstrated his remarkable skills at organization, navi-

Upon returning from his exploits, Drake is knighted by Queen Elizabeth I on the deck of the Golden Hind.

gation, and diplomacy against his sworn enemies. He had lost only seventeen men from his original crew on the *Golden Hind* to disease and skirmishes with the Spanish. Even the New World captains whose treasure he had appropriated described him as courteous, generous, and gallant. The Spanish government, however, was incensed by his activities and petitioned Elizabeth to renounce him as a pirate and to return their treasure.

The queen soon showed she had no intention of doing either. When Drake reached Plymouth, he sent word to Elizabeth that he had returned. When he sailed into London in November, she came on board and knighted Drake for his efforts. Thereafter, he was known as Sir Francis Drake. The *Golden Hind*'s cargo of gold, silver, cloves, and gems was divided among the royal treasury, Drake's investors, and Drake himself. It is impossible to know the exact value of the treasure, but according to Morison, the investors "who paid for outfitting the fleet at an estimated cost of £4,000, were said to have received 1000 per cent on their investment."[49]

In retrospect Drake and his men charted less new territory than had Magellan. He did, however, demonstrate that it was possible to repeat Magellan's feat. His voyage helped diminish some of the fear of such a journey that had been inherent among mariners for generations. Within the next twenty-five years, four more voyages circled the globe. Yet, at the same time, many geographers and explorers alike wondered whether a shorter route from Europe to Asia might exist at the opposite end of the New World from the Strait of Magellan and Cape Horn. Certainly the discovery of such a route would bring untold riches and glory to an intrepid mariner and his nation.

Chapter Four

The Search for the Northwest Passage

For as long as tales of the riches of Cathay and Cipangu existed, adventurers dreamed of finding a direct and easy route to them. Once the voyages of Columbus and others demonstrated that a new and separate landmass lay between Europe and the East, explorers theorized that a water passage existed across the top of the Americas.

The search for this Northwest Passage became more important as voyage after voyage along the Spanish Main and the east coast of South America yielded no shortcuts to the Indies. Even before Christopher Columbus made his final voyage to the New World, explorers were sailing along these new shores in hopes of finding what he had not. One of the first was a fellow Italian who, like Columbus, offered his skills to a foreign king. His original name in Italian is often written as Giovanni Caboto, but he is better known by his Anglicized name of John Cabot.

John Cabot

Very little is known about Cabot's early years. Historians surmise he was born around 1450 in Italy and that he worked as a sailor and navigator involved in the Mediterranean spice trade through the Middle East. He also seems to have been well acquainted with the tales of Marco Polo. Records suggest he was working in Valencia, Spain, in 1493 when Columbus returned from his first voyage with the claim that he had sailed to Cathay (China). Historian R.A. Skelton theorizes that "if John Cabot in fact witnessed the return of Columbus in the spring of 1493, his reading of Marco Polo may well have led him to discredit Columbus' belief that he had reached Cathay, and to suppose that the western sea route to Asia remained to be discovered."[50] His search for sponsors for such a voyage of discovery eventually took him to England, where he received a grant from King Henry VII in 1496. According to the grant, he was permitted to sail "to all parts, regions and coasts of the eastern, western and northern sea, under our banners, flags and ensigns . . . to find, discover and investigate whatsoever islands, countries, regions or provinces . . . in whatsoever part of the world placed, which before this time were unknown to all Christians."[51]

In May 1497 Cabot set out across the Atlantic in a small ship called the *Mathew* with a crew of eighteen, and they made landfall on an unknown shore. He sailed along a coastline teeming with fish and peered through breaks in the fog to observe a heavily timbered land before finding himself back in deep ocean water. Neither Cabot nor anyone else on board the *Mathew*, however, seems to have kept a record of the voyage. Historians have pieced together the voyage based on four surviving letters, none of which is from any of the participants. Because details vary among the letters, the actual location of Cabot's landfall remains subject to debate. Most historians believe it was somewhere in Atlantic Canada, perhaps in the province of Newfoundland and Labrador.

Samuel Eliot Morison speculates that at this point, Cabot turned and sailed back to Europe. According to Morison, "The wind may have blown hard from the west—it generally does at that season. Keeping in mind that Cabot was primarily looking for a passage to the Indies, he would have now felt that he had found it. Regarding this voyage as a mere reconnaissance to prepare for a big expedition later, he decided to turn back."[52]

An artist imagines John Cabot's landing along the Canadian coast of Newfoundland in 1497.

Alwyn Ruddock and the Mystery of John Cabot

Historians have long surmised that when John Cabot and his men disappeared in 1498, they had been lost at sea. In the 1990s, however, a well-respected British maritime historian named Alwyn Ruddock declared that she had found evidence in historical records showing that Cabot had survived. According to Ruddock, Cabot had sailed along the entire eastern coast of North America and reached the Spanish territories in the Caribbean before retracing his route and returning to England in 1500.

Maritime scholars awaited publication of her decades of research with great anticipation. She submitted a summary of her findings to a publisher in 1992, but she died in 2005 before she could publish her work. Her will stipulated that all her papers be destroyed upon her death.

Today historians are trying to find what she had discovered, using her book proposal as a guide. The University of Bristol's Evan T. Jones writes, "Ruddock appears to have made more progress in her research on the voyages of John Cabot than any other historian. If her claims can be validated, she may yet be remembered as one of the greatest scholars to have worked in the field of discovery history. It is almost certainly the case, however, that she will also be remembered as one of the most peculiar."

Evan T. Jones. "Alwyn Ruddock: 'John Cabot and the Discovery of America.'" *Historical Research*, May 2008. http://onlinelibrary.wiley.com/doi/10.1111/j.1468-2281.2007.00422.x/full.

Cabot returned to England with tales of a land with forests of tall, straight trees suitable for ships' masts and shores with fish to feed thousands. Although there was no gold or other treasure, the results of the voyage apparently convinced Henry to sponsor another the following year. Cabot embarked from England in May 1498 with a flotilla of five ships. Two months later, one of his ships arrived in a port in Ireland in dire need of repairs; the other four and Cabot had vanished without a trace.

Jacques Cartier

For the next thirty years, most European voyages to the waters Cabot explored were commercial ventures. English, Portuguese, and French sailors returned with holds filled with the bounty of cod and other fish. One of these Frenchmen was named Jacques Cartier. He wondered whether the Northwest Passage might exist beyond the fishing grounds, and in 1532 he was introduced to François I, the king of France. Cartier proposed an expedition to look for the

Northwest Passage and for sources of precious metals. The king agreed to provide expenses for equipment, provisions, and wages for the voyage.

Cartier sailed from France with two ships on April 20, 1534. The expedition reached the fishing grounds after a swift voyage of twenty days. From there, Cartier and his men circled modern-day Newfoundland and then sailed west, reaching today's Prince Edward Island on June 29. Cartier wrote that the land was filled with "marvelously beautiful and sweet-smelling [trees, such as] cedar, yew, pine, white elm, ash, willow, and several others unknown to us."[53] They crossed to the eastern shore of modern-day New Brunswick, and on July 2 they entered a bay with a wide mouth; because they could not see land at the far end, Cartier hoped this was the entrance to the fabled passage. A group of men rowed into it, and they returned after traveling 80 miles (129km), reporting that it was a bay. Cartier wrote that the week of investigation dashed their hopes and "gave us grief and displeasure."[54] They continued northward along the modern-day Gaspé Peninsula and encountered late summer storms and fog. In a passage they called Détroit de Saint-Pierre (Saint Peter Strait), they saw mountains to the north and encountered contrary currents and tides. There they voted to return to France on August 1, 1534.

Cartier's Second Voyage

When Cartier and his men returned to France in early September, they had good reason to be pleased with their accomplishments. They had spent five months investigating what existed beyond the fishing grounds. They had made contact with native people who eagerly traded their furs for knives, bells, and other European goods, and two young men had joined Cartier for the return to France. They had found no legendary passage to Cathay, but they thought the Saint Peter Strait was worth further investigation. François commissioned Cartier to continue his search. The explorer departed on May 19, 1535, with three ships.

Cartier discovered that the Saint Peter Strait was actually part of a much wider body of water. His native informants told him that it was the mouth of a great river called Hochelaga that spanned "such a distance that no man has been to the end, so far as they had heard say; and no other passage was there except for boats."[55] The informants also said that it was the entrance to a kingdom of great riches called Saguenay. The river is now known as the Saint Lawrence, and today, with the help of modern locks and dams, it provides access to the Great Lakes.

The Frenchmen sailed inland and in September reached a village called Stadacona, near the site of modern-day Quebec City. They reunited the two native men with their father, a local chief. Cartier continued upriver and reached a larger native village on October 2, whose occupants joyously welcomed the explorers. The next day Cartier and his men climbed the tallest hill in the area,

Frenchman Jacques Cartier made three exploratory expeditions to North America, sailing up the St. Lawrence River and establishing an early French colony in Canada.

which he called Mont Royal, and saw that the way upriver was blocked by a series of rapids. The inhabitants of this village, the site of present-day Montreal, convinced him that Saguenay lay farther northwest.

Cartier and his men returned to Stadacona to build a fort and spend the winter. With the assistance of local inhabitants, they survived an outbreak of scurvy by boiling the bark of the arborvitae tree. In May 1536 Cartier returned to France, convinced that the rapids he had seen on the river were the gateway to Saguenay, which he had been led to believe might rival the riches of Peru.

Final Voyage

Cartier began preparations for a third voyage in 1538. The king instructed him to find Saguenay and create a colony on the banks of the Saint Lawrence River. The king, however, placed a royal favorite, Jean-François de Roberval, in charge of the overall expedition, which put Cartier in a position subordinate to the younger Roberval. Cartier was prepared to sail in May 1541, but Roberval was not. He ordered Cartier to go ahead, and on May 23 five vessels with colonists, livestock, and seeds for planting departed for what was now called New France.

In September Cartier chose a site upriver from Stadacona for the settlement. While the colonists built a fort, he went looking for Saguenay. He and his men negotiated the rapids he had seen from Mont Royal but were then defeated by another set upriver. They retreated to the colony, where relations with the local inhabitants had deteriorated. Conditions did not improve during the following winter. Thirty-five of the colonists were killed in skirmishes with the inhabitants. Another outbreak of scurvy was eased by the arborvitae cure, but by spring Cartier was convinced that Roberval was not coming or had been lost at sea. In early June 1542 he and the remaining colonists abandoned their site and sailed downriver. They met Roberval's fleet in the harbor of modern-day Saint John's, Newfoundland, along with dozens of fishing vessels. Cartier returned to France while Roberval continued, determined to create a permanent colony with the men and women he had on board. But his attempt was also abandoned after the following winter.

Cartier never returned to the New World. His efforts, however, contributed to the increasing European knowledge base of North America. Cartographers created new maps, showing the islands of Atlantic Canada and the Saint Lawrence River, but the lands to the north remained a mystery. Perhaps the Northwest Passage could be found there.

Martin Frobisher

English mariners returned to the hunt for the Northwest Passage in the late 1570s. Martin Frobisher had been dreaming of finding a shorter route to the Indies for many years. A shipmate, George Best, wrote that Frobisher was convinced that "a new and nearer passage"[56] existed to Cathay than around the Cape of Good Hope. With the financial backing of the Earl of Warwick and other wealthy men, Frobisher sailed north from England in June 1576 with three ships. The smallest ship was lost in a gale, and another deserted the expedition in July off the coast of Greenland.

Frobisher pressed on without them, in Best's words, "knowing that the sea at length must needs have an ending, and that some land should have a beginning that way."[57] On July 20 they sighted land and sailed north, where they found a great bay that seemed to separate two landmasses. He sailed into it for some 150 miles (240km), convinced that the "land uppon hys right hande as hee sayled [sailed] westward [was] the continente of Asia, and there to bee devided from the firme [mainland] of America, whiche lyeth upon the lefte hande."[58] He named the waterway Frobisher Strait, believing that it mimicked the Strait of Magellan at the southern end of the continent.

After a month of exploring, and losing five crewmen to an encounter with native inhabitants, Frobisher headed back to England. He took along a piece

English explorer Martin Frobisher made three voyages in an attempt to find the Northwest Passage.

of black stone he thought might contain gold ore. After his return in October, two scientists tested the stone and found it to be iron pyrite, or fool's gold—a common and therefore worthless find. Two others disagreed and attested that it contained genuine gold. That news spurred further interest in the expedition, and Frobisher prepared to lead another voyage to his strait.

Second and Third Voyages

The prospect of finding rich gold deposits brought new investors to a venture called the Company of Cathay, which raised funds for a second voyage. In May 1577 Frobisher left with five ships and returned to Frobisher Strait. Queen Elizabeth I directed him to forgo looking for the Northwest Passage on this voyage in favor of mining the ore. Once the fleet reached the strait in July, the crew spent several weeks collecting about 200 tons (181t) of the supposed gold-bearing rock and loading it in their ships before setting sail for England on August 23.

The company's scientists found the ore to be valuable enough that investors backed a third voyage. This time a fleet of fifteen vessels was put at Frobisher's disposal. The company directed him to return for more ore and to bring back 800 tons (726t). In Morison's view, "Absolutely nothing is said about pursuing the northern waters further west; in their greed for gold, the adventurers seem to have forgotten about that passage to Cathay."[59] At the same time, Frobisher was instructed to prepare a group of one hundred men to be left behind with enough provisions for eighteen months.

The fleet left England in May 1578 and reached the strait in July. A storm drove the ships south, and when the weather cleared, the crew members discovered they were seeing a new body of water that Frobisher called the Mistaken Strait, as he had at first believed it was Frobisher Strait. They sailed up it for twenty days before heavy ice forced them to retreat. Frobisher returned to the territory he knew best, and his men began to excavate the ore, but by the end of July the chilly summer was turning cold. A snowstorm dropped more than 6 inches (15cm) of snow on the ships, soaking the men to the skin. The crew abandoned the idea of leaving a party of men behind, and at the end of August they made for home. The ships straggled into England one by one by the start of October, and to the disgust of the investors, the ore inside them was worthless.

Frobisher made no further attempts to find the Northwest Passage. The Company of Cathay went bankrupt, and many of the members of the expedition remained unpaid. Accusations of mismanagement flew back and forth between investors and company officers; because Elizabeth had provided funds for the venture, all documents related to it have been well preserved for generations of historians to examine. Additionally, George Best's narrative of the voyages survives and includes a map of the world that connects Frobisher Strait to a passage to the Pacific. The idea of a Northwest Passage was still alive.

John Davis

Less than ten years after Frobisher's voyages, another Englishman took up the challenge of finding the Northwest Passage. John Davis was a successful privateer and ship's captain, and in February 1585 a group of investors backed his proposal to renew the search for the passage. By June Davis was ready to sail with two ships, the *Sunshine* and the *Moonshine*. In July his ships reached the east coast of Greenland. Davis and his crew rounded its southern tip and sailed northwestward before sighting land to the northeast at the site of the modern-day settlement of Nuuk, Greenland.

They met and traded with native inhabitants before sailing west across open water and reaching land along modern-day Baffin Island. Today this stretch of water is called Davis Strait in the explorer's honor. He followed the coast south until the expedition rounded a cape and found a large gulf. John Janes, a merchant traveling with Davis, left an account of the voyage. He wrote that when the fog lifted on August 11, "we perceived that we were shotte into a very fayre enterance [fair entrance] or passage, being in some places 20 leagues [60 miles or 97km] broade, and in some 30 leagues [90 miles or 145km], altogether voyde of any pester of yce [free of ice], the weather very tollerable, and the water of the very colour, nature and qualite of the mayne [open] ocean, which gave us the greater hope of [making] our passage."[60]

The ships sailed approximately 180 miles (290km) up the passage, which

The Marooning of Marguerite de La Rocque

In 1542 Jean-François de Roberval recruited men and women to join his colonizing efforts in the New World. One of the women, Marguerite de La Rocque, was young and single and joined the expedition along with her nurse, Damienne, and a young man whose name is lost to history. During the voyage La Rocque and the young man were discovered to be lovers. Roberval was incensed and marooned La Rocque, Damienne, and the young man on a deserted island with some food, ammunition, and firearms.

The young man died during the following winter, and Damienne died the following year, leaving La Rocque alone. She survived the best she could until she was rescued by French fishermen in the spring of 1544, after almost two and a half years on the island. She returned to France with them. She told her story to the French historian André Thévet, who recounted her tale in his collection of stories about early Canada.

Today historians believe that La Rocque and her companions were marooned on Harrington Island, one of a group of islands off the coast of southern Quebec in the Gulf of Saint Lawrence. Local tradition holds that she sheltered in a cavern called Marguerite's Cave.

Davis named Cumberland Sound in honor of the Earl of Cumberland. The farther Davis and his crew went, the more they thought that this could be the fabled passage. The water remained deep and ocean-like, they sighted whales coming from the west, and the tidal currents were swift and powerful. But Davis had no desire to tarry and risk the onset of winter, so the two ships returned to England with their news of discovery.

Second and Third Voyages

Davis's second voyage, in the summer of 1586, was less successful than the first. Two ships of his fleet of four voyaged north between Iceland and Greenland to try to find a water route over the North Pole but were turned back by the permanent ice pack. Davis sailed again in the *Moonshine* and ventured farther north along Greenland's coast before crossing Davis Strait in early August and sailing south. He missed Cumberland Sound and eventually made landfall among the islands at the head of Frobisher Strait. He continued south along the coast of Labrador for almost a month before setting sail for England in mid-September.

Davis's investors had confidence in him and financed a third voyage for 1587. He sailed to the north along the west coast of Greenland and reached a point of land he called Hope Sanderson in honor of one of his backers. He turned west and encountered a long wall of ice running from north to south; prevailing winds kept him from sailing around its northern edge, so he turned south. Once he found the southern edge of it, he discovered he was near Cumberland Sound. This time, he discovered that the waterway was a dead end.

The expedition continued down the coast at the beginning of August, passing another gulf where, according to Janes, "the water [was] whirling and roaring, as it were the meeting of tydes."[61] This marked another possible passage, but Davis could not investigate it due to ice. The coast of Labrador began at the gulf's southern edge; Davis retraced his route from the previous year before returning to England.

Davis's attempts to find the Northwest Passage ended with this voyage. His legacy lies in his skill in navigation; his estimates of latitude and distances traveled are remarkably accurate for the time. For example, Morison notes that during Davis's second voyage, "the crossing [from Greenland to Baffin Island] he estimated to be 210 miles, which is nearly correct, and the latitude 66°19', which is less than twenty miles out [from the actual latitude]."[62] Additionally, he noted what he could not explore, leading additional adventurers to sail in his wake. One of the first to do so was a fellow countryman named Henry Hudson.

Henry Hudson

Hudson was born in England around 1570, and no written record of him exists until he became an Arctic explorer. By that time he was apparently a skilled and veteran sea captain. In 1607 he led an expedition to Arctic waters in search of routes over the North Pole; in 1608 he led one in search of a Northeast Passage across the north coast of Asia. Both encountered impenetrable ice and failed in their quests.

Hudson was undeterred, and when he could find no backers in England for a repeat voyage, he contracted with the Dutch East India Company to try to sail to the Indies via a northeast route. In April 1609 he sailed from Amsterdam in Netherlands on board the *Halve Maen* (in English, *Half Moon*) into Norwegian waters before encountering ice. Instead of returning to Amsterdam, he offered the mixed Dutch and English crew an alternative. He showed them letters and a map from his friend Captain John Smith of the Jamestown colony in modern-day Virginia. Smith's letter said that neighboring American Indians convinced him that a Northwest Passage existed in his vicinity. Hudson suggested to his crew members that they continue their voyage in America. The men agreed, and in early July they reached the Newfoundland coast. They sailed south along the east coast as far as today's North Carolina coast before turning north again. Hudson chose not to visit his friends when his ships reached the vicinity of the Jamestown colony, as the *Halve Maen* was a Dutch vessel, and England and Netherlands were seafaring rivals.

On September 3 Hudson and his crew reached a bay with a wide river emptying into it. Hoping that it would lead to the Northwest Passage, they sailed up it for almost a month before it became too shallow for the ship to go farther. Along the way they met and traded with American Indians for fresh fish, shellfish, and vegetables in return for metal objects and cloth. Today this river is named the Hudson River for the *Halve Maen*'s captain. Historians believe that Hudson and his crew navigated it from its mouth, near modern-day New York City, to the area near Albany, New York. Once they returned to open water, they sailed for England, where they arrived on November 7, 1609.

English navigator Henry Hudson sailed for almost a month up today's Hudson River in 1609 and explored the Arctic bay that now bears his name in 1610.

Hudson in the Arctic

It is unclear why Hudson decided to dock in England rather than in Netherlands. Historians speculate that he did not want to face the consequences of breaking his contract for the voyage. The English did not treat him very kindly and imprisoned him for a time. English officials sent his records and log books to Netherlands, and they have been lost to history. In 1610, however, an English trading company agreed to engage Hudson for a new voyage. In April he and twenty men sailed from England in the *Discovery* with the express purpose of finding the Northwest Passage. On board was Hudson's teenage son John, who had been with him on previous journeys, and five sailors from the *Halve Maen* expedition, including Robert Juet, his former navigator.

Things went poorly from the start. Fights broke out among the crew members. Juet accused Hudson of planting a spy among the men, and Hudson threatened to have him put ashore on Iceland. They had reached the Labrador coast by July, and Hudson sailed into the large gulf that Davis had passed on his third voyage. Continuing westward, in August Hudson found a huge body of water to the south. They sailed into it, hoping it was part of the fabled passage. In fact, it is a large bay today called Hudson Bay.

Hudson and his men sailed along its eastern shore, finding bays and islands but no outlet. One of Hudson's crew, Abacuck Prickett, wrote a summary of the expedition in which he lamented that they spent "three months in a labyrinth without end"[63] until the end of October, at which point they decided to beach the *Discovery* and spend the winter there. Within a week they were surrounded by ice. From November 1610 to May 1611, they suffered from lack of food and from scurvy. More arguments between Hudson and his men ensued. Eventually, the ice broke, but the men's discontent did not end with the spring. The ship was caught in ice again, the food supply was almost exhausted, and several men, including Juet, led a mutiny against Hudson. The captain was put in an open boat with his son and seven other men and sent adrift. They were never seen again.

Many of the mutineers died before reaching England. Four of the ringleaders died in a confrontation with several Inuit at the head of Hudson Bay, and Juet died during the return voyage. By the time they reached home, only eight men were left alive. It was an ignominious end to an expedition that added new landmarks to European maps of North America. One of the survivors, Robert Bylot, returned to the Arctic on board the *Discovery* once more. This time the expedition's leader was William Baffin.

William Baffin

Baffin's early life, like Hudson's, is a mystery; however, by 1612 he was an established ship's captain. He was hired in 1615 by a fur-trading company to continue the search for the Northwest Passage. With Bylot as his pilot, and using Hudson's ship, the *Discovery*, he departed England in March 1615 and entered Hudson Strait in June.

Rather than following the southern coast of the strait, which led to Hudson Bay, he followed the northern coast. Baffin found open water to the northwest, and wrote that "this put us in great hope of a passage this waye. . . . There our sudden hopes weare as soon quayld [dashed], for the next morning . . . we sawe the lande trending . . . by the west tyll it bore north-east and by east, and very thick pestred [filled] with ice. . . . We seeing this, soone resolved theare could be no passage in this place . . . and turned the ships head to the southward."[64]

Baffin returned to England in September without the loss of a single man. He was convinced that Hudson Strait was a dead end and would not lead to the Indies. Instead, in a postscript to his report to his employers, he expressed the opinion that exploring the Davis Strait would be more worthwhile. The company agreed, and Baffin prepared for a new expedition for 1616.

"Our Hope of Passage Began to Be Less Every Day"

Once again on board the *Discovery*, Baffin sailed from England in March 1616 and retraced Davis's route up the west coast of Greenland. He passed Hope Sanderson, the farthest north that Davis had achieved, in May and continued up the coast. On July 5 Baffin reached an area of open water he named Smith Sound, after one of the voyage's investors. He was now some 300 miles (483km) farther

north than Davis had been, but ice prevented any further progress.

He and his crew sailed westward and found two more bays of interest, which they also named for investors: Jones Sound and Lancaster Sound. From that point, the amount of ice along the shoreline forced them to sail farther out to sea to the east, and in Baffin's words, "our hope of passage began to be less every day than the other."[65] By the end of July, they were near Cumberland Sound, which they knew to be a dead end. Baffin decided to make for Greenland in hopes of finding a wild herb called scurvy grass to help relieve the crew's scurvy. Once ashore, they collected an abundance of it and boiled it in beer. The concoction worked, and the men regained their health. They returned to England at the end of August.

Baffin's voyages failed to find a Northwest Passage, and after this journey, he was convinced that none existed north of Davis Strait. He told his sponsors that he had sailed almost completely around the strait and now believed that it was merely a great bay. Modern historians and geographers, however, note that he accomplished a great deal even without finding a passage. They note his excellent work in navigation and in accurately measuring latitude. He also diligently recorded the magnetic variations of his compasses throughout his voyages, which helped contribute to the understanding of the earth's magnetic field. Today his achievements are recognized by Baffin Island (the large island bordered on the north by

A map from 1662 shows Hudson's Strait, Hudson's Bay, and Baffin's Bay.

Lancaster Sound and on the south by Hudson Strait, containing Cumberland Sound and Frobisher Bay) and by Baffin Bay (the gulf that lies at the north end of Davis Strait).

Thomas James and Luke Foxe

The search for the Northwest Passage languished for several years following Baffin's voyages. Yet in 1631 not one but two Englishmen set out to explore Hudson Bay in search of the legendary strait. Thomas James's voyage was financed by merchants from the port of Bristol; Luke Foxe was sailing under the royal sponsorship of King Charles I. Both carried provisions for eighteen months, and they departed from England within a few days of each other. Both wrote books about their adventures. But here their similarities end. James was an educated mariner who assembled all the books and maps on the subject he could find; Foxe saw himself as a practical, hands-on seaman and had wanted to find the passage for more than twenty years.

James set sail from Bristol on May 3, 1631, and Foxe left from London on May 5. Both expeditions endured poor weather, ice, and fog during their passages through Hudson Strait. Foxe's instructions from the king were to sail from the western end of the strait to the northwest, but ice prevented him from doing so. From there, he sailed down the western edge of Hudson Bay in late July and early August. He spent two weeks in August making repairs before sailing eastward along the yet-unexplored southwestern shore of the bay.

His ship was favored with excellent weather, and Foxe's book shows that he and his crew were astute observers of the environment around them. British historian Miller Christy records that Foxe "mentions no fewer than twenty-three species of plants, shrubs and trees; twenty-one of mammals; twenty of birds; and several of fish. He also took note of the burial-places and weapons of the natives, though of the natives themselves he saw nothing."[66] Although Foxe saw nothing of the land's original inhabitants, he did encounter his rival, James, in southern Hudson Bay. James had been delayed in reaching the area by ice off Greenland but had taken the same route to the southern part of the bay. There the two ships met on August 29, 1631.

Two Men, One Conclusion

James hosted Foxe for dinner on the evening of August 29. James shared his plans to winter over and to continue searching the following year, and he invited Foxe to join him. Foxe declined and they went their separate ways. Foxe sailed north along the east coast of Hudson Bay and crossed Hudson Strait, passing through a body of water now named Foxe Channel in his honor. He skirted the southwestern edge of Baffin Island and passed into a gulf between it and the Canadian mainland, now called Foxe Basin. His northward trek was halted by ice, and he returned to England on October 31, 1631. He had not lost a single man to injury or disease, which was a remarkable record for explorations in his or any century.

Meanwhile, James sailed south from their rendezvous into a bay that extends from the southeastern corner of Hudson Bay, which today is called James Bay in his honor. He and his crew made a campsite in a forest and endured several months of deep cold and deprivation; four men of their crew of twenty died. They finally broke camp in July

Scurvy

The vitamin C deficiency called scurvy was the bane of many expeditions during the Age of Exploration. Humans cannot create vitamin C in their bodies; it must be absorbed through diet. Scurvy ravaged expeditions that went weeks and months without fresh food. Samuel de Champlain described it in 1613:

> There developed in the mouths of those who had it, large pieces of excess fungus flesh which caused a great rot . . . they could hardly eat anything except in very liquid form. Their teeth barely held in place, and could be removed with the fingers without causing pain. This excess flesh was often cut away, which caused them to bleed extensively from the mouth. Afterwards, severe pain developed in the arms and legs . . .they had almost no strength and suffered unbearable pain. They also had severe cramps in the loins, stomach and bowels, together with a very bad cough and shortness of breath. Unfortunately, we could find no remedy with which to cure these symptoms.

> Scurvy is not contagious, but once one crew member showed signs of the disease, others usually came down with it shortly thereafter, as the men had the same diet. The disease was particularly prominent in expeditions to northern latitudes. A diet that includes fresh meat can help prevent scurvy, but only sources high in vitamin C, such as fresh fruit, can cure the disease. Explorers in search of the Northwest Passage who contracted the disease on board ship often died later, even after reaching land and having access to fresh meat, because few sources of vitamin C grew in the Arctic.

Quoted in Parks Canada: Saint Croix Island International Historic Site. "Champlain's Description of Scurvy." www.pc.gc.ca/eng/lhn-nhs/nb/stcroix/natcul/natcul8.aspx.

but encountered so much ice they did not get to Hudson Bay until August and to Hudson Strait until September. They arrived back in Bristol on September 22, 1632.

The legacies of the James and Foxe voyages extend beyond their names on modern maps. Foxe's book of his expedition begins with a lengthy summary of other Arctic explorations before recounting his own expedition. James recounted only his own voyage, and his narrative style differs greatly from Foxe's. James's book reads almost like a modern adventure novel, as the ship and the crew seem to be constantly in danger. For example, during the winter encampment, James described the deep cold aboard their beached ship as "so extreme [that] no Cloathes were proof against it; no motion could resist it. It would . . . so freeze the haire on our eye-lids, that we could not see: and I verily believe, that it would have stifled [killed] a man, in a very few hours."[67] Despite their different styles, both authors agreed that it was unlikely that the Northwest Passage existed, at least one that could be accessed by way of Hudson Strait. It brought an end to efforts to find the fabled strait during the seventeenth century.

While the exploration of the northern reaches of the New World stagnated, to the south, exploration of the interior was well under way. With the coastlines well documented, Europeans began to move inland. They were motivated by new and amazing tales of untold riches as well as by a desire to claim new territories for their monarchs. In so doing they helped fill in some of the blank spots on their maps of the world.

Chapter Five

Over the Horizon

By the dawn of the seventeenth century, European explorers had visited the coastlines of most of the world's continents. Adventurers had reached India and China and the islands of Japan, visited the Philippines and Indonesia in the East, and sailed along the shores of North and South America. Each new map added new landmarks discovered for European geography, becoming more accurate representations of the world around them. The mythical lands that were featured on maps by Ptolemy and his successors were replaced by territories newly visited and explored. For example, even after Magellan's crew circled the globe, a rumor of a vast southern continent below Africa, South America, and the Indies persisted. This rumor was partly laid to rest in 1642 when the Dutch navigator Abel Tasman proved that lands sighted south of the Indies were, in fact, part of a separate landmass now called Australia.

Now the Europeans began to push inland from the coastal harbors and rivers. They followed waterways, crossed mountains and deserts, and interacted with the native populations with both positive and negative results. In so doing they helped replace speculation with observation and fill in the blanks of the world's terra incognita. One of the first to do so was a Spanish conquistador named Hernando de Soto.

Hernando de Soto

By 1538 de Soto had already had an adventurous career, including marching with Pizarro during the conquest of the Inca. After he was named governor of Cuba and administrator of Florida, he organized an expedition that was designed to impose Spanish rule on Florida. He planned to establish colonies and acquire the treasures that the native peoples were rumored to have. His venture had close to seven hundred soldiers, about one hundred cooks and other support personnel, eight clergy members, an unknown number of slaves, and artisans such as blacksmiths and carpenters. Additionally, he had over two hundred horses, untold numbers of pigs for food, and large dogs designed to attack hostile locals. The party landed in the vicinity of today's Tampa, Florida, in May 1539.

Following rumors of gold, the Spaniards moved north through modern-day Georgia and into present-day South Carolina. Along the way they met a variety of American Indian groups. Few had any treasure for the Spaniards to plunder. One exception was the nation called Cofitachequi. In the spring of 1540, near present-day Camden, South Carolina, the female ruler of Cofitachequi welcomed them and presented them with strings of freshwater pearls. The Spaniards looted native burial sites for more. According to historian David Lavender, "They were not very good pearls and had been discolored by being bored with redhot copper spindles. But they were the closest things to treasure the men had found so far, and De Soto filled a cane chest with 350 pounds of them."[68] Following more rumors of rich native nations, they followed Indian trails into modern-day North Carolina and across the Appalachian Mountains into modern-day Tennessee before following a river south into Alabama.

Throughout the expedition, de Soto's strategy was to march into a village, take the leader and others hostage, and then demand provisions. When the Spanish moved on, the hostages came along to the next settlement and were allowed to go home when that village surrendered. The tactics often worked, but in some cases the local people bristled at the demands and tried to fight. In one confrontation in October 1540, de Soto and his men wiped out an entire fortified town and burned it to the ground. An eyewitness to the carnage wrote, "The whole number of Indians that died in this town, were two thousand and five hundred, little more or less. Of the Christians there died eighteen. . . . Besides those that were slain, there were a hundred and fifty [Spanish] wounded with 700 wounds [from Indian] arrows."[69] De Soto and his men nursed their injuries for almost a month in the vicinity of the burned-out town before proceeding north and camping for the winter in northern Mississippi.

Death Along the Mississippi River

In the spring of 1541, de Soto and his entourage moved north and reached the Mississippi River near present-day Memphis, Tennessee, in early May 1541. One of de Soto's party described the river as nearly 1.5 miles (2.4km) wide and "of great depth, and of a strong current; the water was always muddy; there came down the river continually many trees and timber, which the force of the water and stream brought down."[70] It took them thirty days to construct enough barges to transport everyone across. After exploring through modern-day Arkansas that summer and fall, they made another winter camp

A depiction of Hernando de Soto's encounter with Indians along the banks of the Mississippi River in 1541. He died along the river in 1542.

before returning to the Mississippi in the spring of 1542.

De Soto's force was now half of its original number, since disease and desertion had depleted his army. In addition, he was suffering from what historians surmise was malaria. Shortly after the expedition reached the river in southeastern Arkansas, de Soto died on May 21, 1542. His will appointed his field commander, Luís de Moscoso, as his successor. Moscoso and a few men wrapped de Soto's body in blankets, weighed it down with sand, rowed out into the Mississippi, and rolled the corpse into the water.

Moscoso and the men now tried to march to Mexico. They got as far as east-central Texas before giving up and returning to the Mississippi. They spent their fourth winter building ships and barges in order to navigate the river and then sail to Mexico. By July 1543 the fleet was ready. It took them seventeen days to reach the Gulf of Mexico and almost two months to reach Spanish settlements at the Pánuco River in Mexico (near modern-day Tampico). Only 311 Spaniards survived.

In some ways de Soto's expedition was a spectacular failure; the survivors returned with no treasures from native empires, mostly because there were none to be gained. He was a ruthless campaigner against the inhabitants, and his actions set the stage for many interactions with Europeans who came to the region later. Yet he and his men were the first to encounter and observe the landscape and cultures of the American Southeast, and their accounts provide valuable insights into a now-vanished world.

Francisco Vásquez de Coronado

While de Soto and his men were exploring the American Southeast, another Spanish expedition was moving through the American Southwest. Francisco Vásquez de Coronado, the governor of the province of Nueva Galicia in northern Mexico, had heard tales of lands rich with treasure that existed north of Spanish territory. The stories centered on a kingdom called Cibola and its seven cities, one of which was also called Cibola. The kingdom's riches were said to rival that of the Inca and the Aztec. These stories came from a variety of sources, including native traders who traveled an ancient route between Mexico City (the former Tenochtitlán) and unknown territories to the north and from Spanish adventurers who had learned to speak with the local inhabitants. Another source was a Franciscan friar who claimed that he had visited Cibola. Coronado was inspired to investigate.

In February 1540 he moved north from Nueva Galicia with about three hundred soldiers, along with slaves and local inhabitants, over one thousand horses and mules, and a herd of about one thousand cattle, sheep, and goats for food. In April Coronado took a smaller party of about one hundred ahead to reach Cibola while the main body waited for instructions. He rode into present-day Arizona, following rivers northward and crossing mountains, before reaching Cibola in early July. The town turned out to be a crushing disappointment. The people lived in unadorned mud-walled houses and had no caches of gold or silver. The inhabitants called the town Hawikuk. Coronado wrote back to his superiors in Mexico City that the Franciscan friar who had extolled the marvels of Cibola had "not told the truth in a single thing that he said, but that everything is the opposite of what he related, except the name of the cities and the large stone houses."[71]

Coronado remained hopeful that the legendary treasures remained to be found. He sent out scouting parties from Hawikuk to scout the countryside. One party reported what historians believe to be the first European encounter with the Grand Canyon. Others returned without finding any riches but brought new informants to the Spanish camp. One informant was a member of the Pawnee Nation, who told them of the kingdom of Quivira, which lay to the east and which had the riches the Spanish were seeking. Coronado and his men ventured through modern-day New Mexico and across the panhandles of Texas and Oklahoma before entering central Kansas. Along the way, they encountered vast herds of bison, which they called "bulls" or "cattle," and a group of native people they called the Querecho. These people were nomads, following the herds of bison across the land. Historians surmise that they were members of the Apache Nation.

More Disappointments

Coronado pressed on toward Quivira. When he finally reached what his native informant said was Quivira in July 1541, it was as disappointing as Cibola had been. These people were ancestors of

In 1541 Francisco de Coronado led his men across the American Southwest in search of the legendary "Seven Cities of Gold."

the Wichita, and according to Lavender, lived in "a cluster of domed huts built of stout frameworks of logs overlaid with grass, so they looked like haystacks. The surrounding land, rolling and fertile, produced fine corn, pumpkins, and tobacco. But no gold."[72] Coronado stayed among them for several weeks, riding from village to village without finding any treasure. Finally, they headed back to Mexico, arriving in September 1542.

In terms of finding new kingdoms to conquer, Coronado's expedition was as much a failure as de Soto's had been. Coronado, however, survived his adventure. Upon his return to Mexico, he was put on trial for mismanaging the army and for failing to press on past Quivira; he was eventually acquitted of the charges. His health was compromised following a fall from his horse and from the strain of the trial, and he died in September 1554 at age forty-four.

While de Soto and Coronado were wandering through the North American continent, another group of Spaniards was involved in another adventure. This one took place in South America and involved one of the longest rivers in the world.

Francisco de Orellana

In 1540 Francisco Pizarro's half brother Gonzalo enlisted a fellow conquistador named Francisco de Orellana to help investigate another rumor of a rich native empire. This one, called the Land of Cinnamon, was said to be located on the east side of the Andes mountain range from present-day Ecuador. In February 1541 Pizarro and Orellana assembled a force of about 250 Spaniards and 4,000 native inhabitants to cross the mountains. By the time they completed the crossing, they were down to about 130 Spaniards and 1,000 native inhabitants due to disease and desertion.

Pizarro and Orellana soon discovered that the legendary Land of Cinnamon did not exist; all they encountered were endless jungles and scattered villages. But they kept looking. That autumn on the banks of the Coca River, they built a small, open ship to carry supplies and the sick. One group of soldiers guided it downstream while the main body slogged on foot through the dense jungle, fording creeks and tributaries and trying to keep up with the boat.

By December the men were exhausted and malnourished. Orellana offered to take the strongest men downriver to find food and return in two weeks. The Coca flowed into the Napo River, and the current became increasingly swift. With each passing day, Orellana believed conditions were making the prospects of a return to Pizarro increasingly slim. After eight days Orellana's party encountered friendly inhabitants at a village called Imara who gave them much-needed food. Orellana and his men realized it would be almost impossible to fight against the strong currents to rejoin Pizarro, so they decided to proceed downriver. They tarried at Imara throughout January 1542; on February 2, now having regained their strength, they returned to the river.

Francisco de Orellana and the Amazons

Gaspar de Carvajal's account of Francisco de Orellana's journey down the Amazon River described a wide variety of native populations. His descriptions were based on firsthand observation and on accounts shared by native peoples with whom they spoke. In one instance the Spanish skirmished with a group of inhabitants that seemed to be led by women. Orellana spoke the next day with a native who was serving as a guide. The young man told Orellana and Carvajal that the women were part of a much larger nation, populated only by females, who lived far to the south of the river and who ruled over a number of groups in the area. The guide's tale included stories of great stone buildings covered in gold and silver in which the women lived, as well as how they used captured prisoners to increase their numbers.

Orellana related his adventure to King Charles V of Spain, who was fascinated by the encounter with and description of the warriors. The king called the river Amazonas after the Amazons, female warriors in Greek mythology. Recent investigators surmise that the warriors were actually men of the Icamiaba Nation whom the Spanish mistook for women.

The Amazon and the Ocean

The Napo flowed into an even larger river, which carried them swiftly downstream. They paused for almost two months at a village called Aparia, where they built a second, larger ship they called the *Victoria* to complement the smaller and cramped *San Pedro*. In May they entered the realm of a leader named Machiparo. Gaspar de Carvajal, who left an account of this voyage, said Machiparo

> dwells on a ridge at the river's edge and rules over many large settlements. . . . Before reaching this settlement, from a distance of two leagues [6 miles or 9.7km], we could see the light color of the villages, and we had not progressed far when a very large number of canoes came upstream, all splendidly fitted for war, with their shields made of lizard skin and of hides of manatees and tapirs, each shield the height of a man, covering him entirely. The warriors raised a loud noise, drumming numerous drums and blowing wooden trumpets, threatening that they would eat us.[73]

Several skirmishes with native inhabitants loyal to Machiparo followed the

Spaniards downriver. Sometimes the Indians attacked from onshore, raining poisoned arrows on the visitors; other times, they rowed out and fought in midstream.

After passing beyond Machiparo's domain, Orellana and his men found that the jungle that had surrounded them since leaving the Andes was giving way to open grassland with scattered clusters of trees. By summer the river was showing signs of tidal activity. They felt they were nearing the ocean, especially as the river became a series of marshes and islands that hid the shorelines from the main channel. On August 26, 1542, they reached the open sea of the Atlantic. They mounted masts on their river craft and turned old clothing into sails. They sailed northwest along the coastline of modern-day Brazil until they reached Spanish settlements in today's Venezuela in mid-September.

Today this river is called the Amazon. Orellana and his men had become the first Europeans to navigate most of its length, from where the Napo joins it to the Atlantic coast. It was an epic journey, but Orellana is less well known than many of his fellow conquistadores. In the opinion of science and nature writer Charles C. Mann, "Neither Orellana's journey nor Carvajal's account received the attention they merited; indeed, Carvajal's work was not formally published until 1894. Part of the reason for the lack of attention is that Orellana didn't conquer anything—he simply managed to emerge with his life."[74] Orellana's expedition was not the first by Europeans to follow a river, but it was one of the first to follow a river downstream to its end. In its wake was a new generation of explorers who took to the rivers of the New World.

Francisco de Orellana's navigation of the Amazon River is one of the most amazing, yet lesser known, accomplishments of the Age of Exploration.

FRANCISCO
DE
ORELLANA
1511-1546

Samuel de Champlain

In the years following the first French explorations in New France, entrepreneurs returned to the area to begin trading with Native Americans for animal furs, such as fox, beaver, and mink. In 1603 Samuel de Champlain arrived in the New World with a fur-trading expedition, and inspired by the voyages of Jacques Cartier sixty years earlier, he sailed down the Saint Lawrence River and met with many of the native groups in the area.

When he returned to France, he published a book with his map. The following year he helped create a colony at present-day Port Royal, Nova Scotia. For the next three years, before the French abandoned it, Champlain sailed to and from Port Royal, exploring and mapping coastlines, islands, and rivers, recording what he saw. His accounts are filled with descriptions of landmarks that are still recognizable four hundred years later. For example, on July 19, 1605, he wrote:

> As we continued our course [south], we saw some land which seemed to us to be islands, but as we came nearer we found it to be the main land, lying to the north-north-west of us, and that it was the cape of a large bay, containing more than eighteen or nineteen leagues [about 55 miles or 89km] in circuit, into which we had run so far that we had to wear off on the other tack [sail north] in order to [round] the cape we had seen.[75]

Champlain had reached the coast of modern-day Massachusetts, sailing in Cape Cod Bay between Cape Cod and the mainland. Additional voyages took him along the coasts of Nova Scotia and Maine before the party returned to France in 1607.

New Beginnings and New Discoveries

In 1608 Champlain returned to New France with a new mission. He was hired by the French company that had a monopoly on the fur trade to create a permanent settlement. In his words there was no place for a settlement "more convenient or better situated than the point of Québec, so called by the [local inhabitants], which was covered by nut trees."[76] He and twenty-seven men prepared to spend the winter in a tiny enclave. They suffered from dysentery and scurvy, and by the time more settlers arrived in the spring, only Champlain and eight others were still alive. But now reinforced, he continued his explorations; in the summer of 1609, he became the first recorded European to visit Lake Champlain, on the border between modern-day Vermont and New York. In 1614 he ventured as far west as Lake Huron, spending a winter among the Native Americans of the region.

The politics of the colony began to occupy more of his time, but he encouraged new arrivals to New France to continue exploring. One, named Jean Nicolet, spent several years as a fur trader among the native inhabitants in modern-day western Ontario, where he

An artist imagines French explorer Samuel de Champlain's 1609 arrival along the shores of the lake that now bears his name.

heard about other tribes that lived to the west and south along the shores of an unknown bay. The native people with whom he lived referred to them by the name "People of the Sea." Nicolet wondered whether these people lived along or near the China Sea. After hearing this tale, Champlain encouraged Nicolet to discover whether it was true.

Jean Nicolet

In 1634 Nicolet set off on his journey to the west and south, fully prepared to meet the People of the Sea. He traveled across Lake Huron, passed through the Straits of Mackinac, and entered today's Lake Michigan. In the words of the seventeenth-century chronicler Barthélemy Vimont, "He wore a grand robe of

China damask, all strewn with flowers and birds of many colors."[77] The people he met called themselves the Hochungara and lived along the shores of today's Green Bay in Wisconsin. They were ancestors of today's Winnebago Nation. They greeted him warmly, but they spoke a language unrelated to that spoken by the eastern woodland Canadian native inhabitants he knew; their language was a dialect of the Siouan language spoken by American Indians who lived farther west.

Nicolet enjoyed their company for several weeks as he traveled up the Fox River that flows into Green Bay as far as Lake Winnebago. Each group of inhabitants tried to outdo the other in holding feasts for him; Vimont relates that "at one of these banquets, they served at least sixscore [120] Beavers."[78] No first-person account of this expedition survives, leaving historians to scour the secondhand accounts to piece together where Nicolet went from there. One supposition is that he traveled south overland to the Illinois River, and another is that he went west and followed the Wisconsin River. Both eventually flow into the Mississippi River. Historian Louise P. Kellogg notes that in 1640, a Jesuit in Quebec recalled a conversation he had with Nicolet. He said Nicolet had told him "that if he had sailed three days' journey farther upon a great river which issues from [Lake Michigan] he would have found the sea."[79] Kellogg surmises that Nicolet was repeating what he had learned from the Winnebago, and that the sea in question was actually the Mississippi River. Regardless, Nicolet does not seem to have seen the Mississippi; he spent the winter with the Winnebago and then returned to Quebec in the fall of 1635. He shared his discoveries with Champlain shortly before the elder explorer died on Christmas Day 1635. Nicolet was the first recorded European to venture into today's Wisconsin, but he never returned after 1635. He spent the following years as a fur trader and died in a boating accident in 1642.

Marquette and Jolliet

By the 1670s French fur traders, settlers, and Catholic missionaries had spread out from the first New France settlements along the Saint Lawrence River to establish towns and trading posts throughout the Great Lakes region. The traders were interested in the profits to be made in purchasing furs from the native inhabitants; the missionaries were dedicated to converting the native peoples to Catholicism. Both groups spent time in the wilderness, learning about the land and the ways of the local inhabitants. Jacques Marquette was a Jesuit missionary working in present-day Wisconsin who heard tales of a great river, called Mississippi, to the west. He enlisted the aid of Louis Jolliet, a French Canadian trader and explorer, to find the river and discover whether it might lead to the Pacific Ocean.

In May 1673 Marquette, Jolliet, and five companions traveled in two canoes up the Fox River and continued overland to the Wisconsin River. In Marquette's words, "After proceeding 40 leagues [120 miles or 200km] on this same route, we arrived at the mouth of our river; and, at 42 and a half degrees of latitude, we safely entered Missisipi on the 17th of June, with a joy that I cannot express."[80] Marquette and Jolliet were not the first Europeans to sight the Mississippi; de Soto and his men had visited it in 1541, but no others had traveled on it in this region. As the river continued flowing to the south, they assumed it would eventually flow into the Gulf of Mexico. Marquette spoke six American Indian languages and noted the native names on the landscape as they passed. Today's Missouri River was called the Pekitanouï, and the Ohio River was called the Ouaboukigou. At a village called Akamsea, they learned that they were now just ten days' journey from the gulf.

Jesuit missionary Jacques Marquette and French-Canadian trader Louis Jolliet explore the Mississippi River in 1673.

At this point, Marquette and Jolliet decided to halt and return upriver. They had already narrowly avoided a confrontation with a group of American Indians who were armed with European firearms, and they did not wish to risk further encounters. Nor did they wish to find themselves suddenly surrounded by Spanish adventurers, who were known to be trading along the gulf coast; Marquette wrote that "the Spaniards . . . without doubt . . . would have at least detained us as captives."[81] They started north on July 17, 1673, and left the Mississippi River to navigate the Illinois River. From there they crossed to Lake Michigan near the site of present-day Chicago, Illinois. Marquette returned to his mission on Green Bay, while Jolliet traveled to Quebec to report their discoveries. Near the end of Jolliet's journey, his canoe overturned and he lost his personal journal of the expedition; however, Marquette's own account, which he wrote after his return to Green Bay, has survived.

René-Robert Cavelier, Sieur de La Salle

Marquette and Jolliet's adventures inspired a number of later French Canadian explorers. The most notable was René-Robert Cavelier, who is better known by his title, Sieur de La Salle (in English, Lord of La Salle, his family's estate in France). He spent a number of years traveling through the Great Lakes and the Illinois River as far south as present-day Peoria, Illinois, where he built an encampment he called Fort

Crèvecoeur. In 1680 he made a cross-country trek from the fort to modern-day Kingston, Ontario, in the dead of winter. By 1682 he was well known in French Canada for his seemingly inexhaustible energy and zeal for exploration. During his travels he learned as much as possible from the native peoples about what existed beyond their territories. Now he was ready for a new adventure: to travel to the mouth of the Mississippi River.

In January 1682 he left Fort Crèvecoeur with twenty-three Frenchmen and eighteen Native Americans; they reached the Mississippi in February. In March they paused in the vicinity of present-day Memphis, Tennessee, for several days and built a small fort while looking for one of their party who had become separated from them while hunting. He reappeared a week later, and they continued downriver. By the end of the month, they had reached the mouth of the Arkansas River and camped among villages of the Quapaw Nation. La Salle's second in command, Henri de Tonti, described the surrounding landscape: "Their country is very beautiful, having abundance of peach, plum, and apple trees. Vines flourish there. Buffaloes, deer, stags, bears, turkeys, are very numerous. They even have domestic fowls. They have very little snow during the winter, and the ice is not thicker than a [coin]."[82]

The party was in the country where Marquette and Jolliet had turned back. La Salle and his men continued downriver and reached the mouth of the river on April 7, 1682. They performed a ceremony in which they declared that they

Niagara Falls

As French traders and missionaries moved along the Great Lakes in the 1600s, they heard tales of spectacular waterfalls along the Niagara River between Lakes Erie and Ontario. The first explorer to publish his observations of the falls was Louis Hennepin in his 1678 work *A New Discovery of a Vast Country in America*. He explained:

> Betwixt the Lake Ontario and Erie, there is a vast and prodigious Cadence of Water which falls down after a surprising and astonishing manner, insomuch that the Universe does not afford its Parallel. It is so rapid above this Decent, that it violently hurries down the wild Beasts while endeavoring to pass it to feed on the other side, they not being able to withstand the force of its Current, which inevitably casts them down headlong above Six hundred foot [183 m]. . . . The Waters which fall from this vast height, do foam and boil after the most hideous manner imaginable, making an outrageous Noise, more terrible than that of Thunder.

Although Hennepin described the geographic setting accurately, he overestimated the height. The tallest of the three falls, called Horseshoe Falls, is about 175 feet (53m) tall.

Louis Hennepin. *A New Discovery of A Vast Country in America*. Vol. 1. Edited by Reuben Gold Thwaites. Chicago: McClurg, 1903, pp. 54–55. www.americanjourneys.org/aj-124a.

Louis Hennepin was the first white man to view and describe Niagara Falls.

were taking possession of the land for France, and La Salle named the territory in honor of French King Louis XIV. Tonti observed that along most of the Mississippi, the riverbanks are "almost uninhabitable, on account of the spring floods" and that there "are but few beavers, but to make amends, there is a large number of buffaloes or bears, large wolves, stags . . . and . . . deer in abundance."[83] The party headed back upriver and reached Lake Michigan in July; La Salle continued to Quebec and then to France to report their discoveries.

La Salle received permission from Louis to return to the mouth of the Mississippi, but the expedition turned out to be a monumental failure. La Salle and a large number of colonists left France in 1684, intending to reach the mouth of the river from the Gulf of Mexico. A variety of miscalculations led them to attempt to settle along the coast of modern-day Texas. La Salle was killed in 1687 by conspirators who rebelled against his command. Tonti found the news distressing, saying, "Such was the end of one of the greatest men of this age, a man of admirable spirit, and capable of undertaking all sorts of explorations."[84] On the other hand, Henri Joutel, who accompanied La Salle on his final expedition, described his excellent qualities as "counterbalanced by too haughty a behavior, which sometimes made him [too rigid] towards those that were under his command."[85] In any case his achievements live on through the name he chose for the Mississippi River territory: Louisiana.

Beyond the Horizon

In many ways La Salle was like many of the adventurous Europeans of the Age of Exploration. He built upon the discoverers who had gone before him, pushing the bounds of recorded knowledge a bit further each time. By the time of La Salle's death in 1687, Europeans had spent 250 years traveling beyond their familiar horizons. They had ventured past Cape Bojador, around the Cape of Good Hope, across the Atlantic Ocean, through the Strait of Magellan, across the Pacific Ocean, and into myriad rivers, bays, and gulfs throughout the Americas, Africa, and Asia.

By the close of the seventeenth century, the perspective of the T-O map was a relic of the past. Maps that placed Europe and the Middle East in the center of the world, surrounded by an impenetrable Sea of Darkness, were as much a part of the past as the legend of Prester John. The maps printed in the early part of the eighteenth century still contained areas of unknown territories; for example, both the Arctic and Antarctic regions remained to be fully charted. The continents, however, had attained the shapes familiar to modern observers. The maps were further refined at the close of the eighteenth century when mariners and scientists learned how to accurately measure longitude, the east-west complement to latitude's north-south method of determining location. Now even the smallest landmark could be accurately charted in relation to a fixed point on the globe. Additionally, enterprising geographers worked with

Lilliput, El Dorado, and the Continuing World of Imagination

The discoveries of the Age of Exploration did not mean that Europeans no longer imagined far-off and unknown lands. Some legendary lands, such as Prester John's kingdom, disappeared from maps, but the lure of and excitement connected with the unknown continued to fire readers' imaginations well after the earth's seas had been charted and the coastlines explored.

Some writers conjured up new lands and described them in relation to known landmarks. In 1726 English author Jonathan Swift published *Gulliver's Travels*, which included a visit to Lilliput. It was a fictional island in the South Indian Ocean, to the south of Sumatra; there the inhabitants were one-twelfth the size of average humans. Other writers kept earlier legends alive. In 1759 French satirist and playwright Voltaire published *Candide*, which featured the legendary city of gold called El Dorado. As the title character wanders through the South American jungle, he stumbles upon El Dorado, where a benevolent king rules over a peaceful land free of money and religion.

The travels of both Candide and Gulliver fired the imaginations of readers everywhere and helped keep alive the lure of adventure and exploration.

printers to create portable atlases that divided up the world into smaller sections for easier reading. As Daniel J. Boorstin puts it, "Interested Europeans could now carry around in their pocket the latest version of the earth."[86]

It remained for later generations of explorers to discover what awaited in the mystical and unknown interiors of Africa and the Americas, whether a Northwest Passage truly existed, and what could be found in Australia and the icy reaches of Antarctica. They ventured forth in the same spirit of discovery as those who had led the way during the Age of Exploration.

Notes

Introduction: Marco Polo and Prester John

1. Daniel J. Boorstin. *The Discoverers*. New York: Random House, 1983, p. 105.

Chapter One: Conquering the "Sea of Darkness"

2. Toby Lester. *The Fourth Part of the World*. New York: Free Press, 2009, p. 31.
3. Boorstin. *The Discoverers*, p. 160.
4. Quoted in Boorstin. *The Discoverers*, p. 161.
5. Quoted in Boorstin. *The Discoverers*, p. 166.
6. Lester. *The Fourth Part of the World*, p. 218.
7. Lester. *The Fourth Part of the World*, p. 226.
8. Boorstin. *The Discoverers*, p. 176.
9. Quoted in Alvaro Velho, João da Sá, and Ernest George Ravenstein. *A Journal of the First Voyage of Vasco da Gama, 1497–1499*. London: Hakluyt Society, 1898, p. 76.
10. Quoted in German Arcienegas. *Why America? 500 Years of a Name; The Life and Times of Amerigo Vespucci*. Bogota, Colombia: Villegas Editores, 2002, p. 184.
11. Quoted in Velho et al. *A Journal of the First Voyage of Vasco da Gama, 1497–1499*, pp. 113–114.
12. Tomés Pires. *The Suma Oriental of Tomés Pires*. Edited by Armando Cortesão. New Delhi, India: Asian Educational Services, 2005, p. lxxiv.
13. Quoted in Pires. *The Suma Oriental of Tomés Pires*, p. lxxix.

Chapter Two: Columbus and the Conquistadores

14. Louis de Vorsey Jr. *Keys to the Encounter: A Library of Congress Resource Guide for the Study of the Age of Discovery*. Washington, DC: Library of Congress, 1992, p. 17.
15. Quoted in Vorsey. *Keys to the Encounter*, p. 17.
16. Quoted in Samuel Eliot Morison. *Admiral of the Ocean Sea: A Life of Christopher Columbus*. Boston: Little, Brown, 1942, p. 71.
17. Samuel Eliot Morison. *The European Discovery of America: The Southern Voyages, A.D. 1492–1616*. New York: Oxford University Press, 1974, pp. 42–43.
18. Quoted in J.M. Cohen, ed. *The Four Voyages of Christopher Columbus*. London: Penguin, 1969, p. 41.
19. Morison. *The European Discovery of America*, p. 57.
20. Quoted in Boorstin. *The Discoverers*, p. 233.
21. Quoted in Lester. *The Fourth Part of the World*, p. 271.

22. J.M. Roberts. *History of the World*. New York: Oxford University Press, 1993, p. 425.
23. Quoted in Lester. *The Fourth Part of the World*, p. 290.
24. Morison. *The European Discovery of America*, p. 503.
25. Quoted in Morison. *The European Discovery of America*, p. 202.
26. Quoted in John Carey, ed. *Eyewitness to History*. Cambridge, MA: Harvard University Press, 1987, p. 83.
27. Bernal Diaz del Castillo. *The Memoirs of the Conquistador Bernal Diaz del Castillo, Written by Himself, Containing a True and Accurate Account of the Discovery and Conquest of Mexico and New Spain*. Translated by John Ingram Lockhart. London: Hatchard, 1844, p. 222.
28. Quoted in William H. Prescott. *The Conquest of Peru*. Morristown, NJ: Digital Antiquaria, 2004, p. 239.
29. Chris Harman. *A People's History of the World*. London: Verso, 2008, p. 169.
30. Harman. *A People's History of the World*, p. 171.
31. Quoted in Harman. *A People's History of the World*, p. 171.

Chapter Three: Around the World

32. Boorstin. *The Discoverers*, p. 260.
33. V.R. LaLonde. "Ferdinand Magellan: Circumnavigating the Globe." European Voyages of Exploration: The Fifteenth and Sixteenth Centuries, Applied History Research Group, University of Calgary, 1997. www.ucalgary.ca/applied_history/tutor/eurvoya/magellan.html.
34. Quoted in Laurence Bergreen. *Over the Edge of the World: Magellan's Terrifying Circumnavigation of the Globe*. HarperCollins e-books, 2008, p. 128.
35. Morison. *The European Discovery of America*, p. 367.
36. Quoted in Bergreen. *Over the Edge of the World*, p. 174.
37. Quoted in Bergreen. *Over the Edge of the World*, p. 175.
38. Morison. *The European Discovery of America*, p. 403.
39. Quoted in Bergreen. *Over the Edge of the World*, p. 214.
40. Morison. *The European Discovery of America*, p. 420.
41. Quoted in Morison. *The European Discovery of America*, p. 428.
42. Quoted in Bergreen. *Over the Edge of the World*, p. 385.
43. Morison. *The European Discovery of America*, p. 634.
44. Quoted in Morison. *The European Discovery of America*, p. 637.
45. Francis Fletcher. *The World Encompassed by Sir Francis Drake, Being His Next Voyage to That of Nombre de Dios: Collated with an Unpublished Manuscript of Francis Fletcher, Chaplain to the Expedition*. London: Hakluyt Society, 1854, p. 234.
46. Quoted in Morison. *The European Discovery of America*, pp. 643–644.
47. Quoted in Morison. *The European Discovery of America*, p. 648.
48. Fletcher. *The World Encompassed by Sir Francis Drake, Being His Next Voyage to That of Nombre de Dios*, p. 225.
49. Morison. *The European Discovery of America*, p. 684.

Chapter Four: The Search for the Northwest Passage

50. R.A. Skelton. "Cabot (Caboto), John (Giovanni)." *Dictionary of Canadian Biography Online*, 2000. www.biographi.ca/009004-119.01-e.php?&id_nbr=101.

51. Quoted in H.B. Biggar, ed. *The Precursors of Jacques Cartier, 1497–1534*. Ottawa: Government Printing Bureau, 1911, p. 8.

52. Samuel Eliot Morison. *The Great Explorers: The European Discovery of America*. New York: Oxford University Press, 1978, p. 66.

53. Quoted in Morison. *The Great Explorers*, p. 197.

54. Quoted in Morison. *The Great Explorers*, p. 200.

55. Quoted in Morison. *The Great Explorers*, p. 219.

56. George Best. *The Three Voyages of Martin Frobisher: In Search of a Passage to Cathaia and India by the North-West*, A.D. *1576–8*. London: Hakluyt Society, 1867, p. 70.

57. Best. *The Three Voyages of Martin Frobisher*, p. 72.

58. Best. *The Three Voyages of Martin Frobisher*, p. 72.

59. Morison. *The Great Explorers*, p. 308.

60. Quoted in Richard Hakluyt. *The Principal Navigations, Voyages, Traffiques & Discoveries of the English Nation, Made by Sea or Over-Land to the Remote and Farthest Distant Quarters of the Earth at Any Time Within the Compass of These 1600 Yeeres*. Vol. 7. Glasgow: MacLehose, 1904, p. 390.

61. Quoted in Hakluyt. *The Principal Navigations, Voyages, Traffiques & Discoveries of the English Nation*, p. 421.

62. Morison. *The Great Explorers*, p. 339.

63. Quoted in G.M. Asher, ed. *Henry Hudson the Navigator: The Original Documents in Which His Career Is Recorded, Collected, Partly Translated, and Annotated*. London: Hakluyt Society, 1860, p. 110.

64. Quoted in Clements R. Markham, ed. *The Voyages of William Baffin, 1612–1622*. London: Hakluyt Society, 1881, pp. 131–132.

65. Quoted in Markham, ed. *The Voyages of William Baffin, 1612–1622*, p. 147.

66. Miller Christy. *Captain Luke Foxe of Hull, and Captain Thomas James of Bristol: In Search of a North-west Passage in 1631–32*. Vol. 1. London: Hakluyt Society, 1894, p. cxxx.

67. Quoted in John Delaney. "Thomas James and Luke Foxe: 1631–1632." Of Maps and Men: In Pursuit of a Northwest Passage, Princeton University Library. http://libweb5.princeton.edu/visual_materials/maps/websites/northwest-passage/james-foxe.htm.

Chapter Five: Over the Horizon

68. David Lavender. *De Soto, Coronado, Cabrillo: Explorers of the Northern Mystery*. Washington, DC: US Department of the Interior, 1992, p. 44.

69. A Gentleman of Elvas. *The Discovery and Conquest of Terra Florida by Don Ferdinando de Soto, and Six Hundred Spaniards His Followers*. Edited by William B. Rye. Translated by

Richard Hakluyt. London: Hakluyt Society, 1851, p. 79.

70. A Gentleman of Elvas. *The Discovery and Conquest of Terra Florida by Don Ferdinando de Soto*, p. 92.

71. Quoted in Vorsey. *Keys to the Encounter*, p. 102.

72. Lavender. *De Soto, Coronado, Cabrillo*, p. 82.

73. Quoted in Frank Salomon and Stuart B. Schwartz, eds. *The Cambridge History of Native Peoples of the Americas: Vol. 3, South America*, Part 1. Cambridge: Cambridge University Press, 1999, pp. 146–147.

74. Charles C. Mann. *1491: New Revelations of the Americas Before Columbus*. New York: Vintage, 2006, p. 320.

75. Samuel de Champlain. *Voyages of Samuel de Champlain*. Translated by Charles Pomeroy Otis. Boston: Prince Society, 1878, p. 79. www.americanjourneys.org/aj-115.

76. Quoted in N.E. Dionne. *Champlain*. Toronto: Morang, 1905, p. 41. http://eco.canadiana.ca/view/oocihm.77420.

77. Barthélemy Vimont. *The Jesuit Relations and Allied Documents: Travels and Explorations of the Jesuit Missionaries in New France, 1610–1791. Vol. 23*. Edited and translated by Reuben Gold Thwaites. Cleveland: Burrows Brothers, 1898, p. 279. http://eco.canadiana.ca/view/oocihm.07557/3?r=0&s=1.

78. Vimont. *The Jesuit Relations and Allied Documents*, p. 279.

79. Quoted in Louise P. Kellogg, ed. *Early Narratives of the Northwest, 1634–1699*. New York: Charles Scribner's Sons, 1917, p. 12. www.Americanjourneys.org/aj-043.

80. Quoted in Kellogg. *Early Narratives of the Northwest, 1634–1699*, p. 236. www.americanjourneys.org/aj-051.

81. Quoted in Kellogg. *Early Narratives of the Northwest, 1634–1699*, p. 256. www.americanjourneys.org/aj-051.

82. Quoted in Kellogg. *Early Narratives of the Northwest, 1634–1699*, p. 298. www.Americanjourneys.org/aj-053.

83. Quoted in Kellogg. *Early Narratives of the Northwest, 1634–1699*, p. 302. www.Americanjourneys.org/aj-053.

84. Quoted in Kellogg. *Early Narratives of the Northwest, 1634–1699*, p. 319. www.Americanjourneys.org/aj-053.

85. Henri Joutel. *A Journal of the Last Voyage Perform'd by Monsr. de la Sale, to the Guelph of Mexico, to Find Out the Mouth of the Missisipi River*. London: Bell, Lintott, and Baker, 1714, p. 100. www.americanjourneys.org/aj-121.

86. Boorstin. *The Discoverers*, p. 278.

For More Information

Books

Laurence Bergreen. *Over the Edge of the World: Magellan's Terrifying Circumnavigation of the World*. New York: HarperCollins, 2003. Adding modern geographic understanding to Magellan's pioneering voyage, Bergreen presents the challenges and hardships endured throughout the journey.

Daniel Boorstin. *The Discoverers*. New York: Random House, 1983. Former Library of Congress historian Boorstin's work, divided into four parts, provides fascinating looks at individuals who changed our perception of the world. Part 2, *The Earth and the Seas*, deals with the Age of Exploration.

Christopher Columbus. *The Four Voyages: Being His Own Log-Book, Letters and Dispatches with Connecting Narratives*. New York: Penguin Classics, 1992. Columbus's voyages, discoveries, and personal opinions in his own words.

Bernal Diaz del Castillo. *The Conquest of New Spain*. New York: Penguin, 1963. An insightful account of the Aztec Empire and its overthrow by Spanish conquistadores by one of the participants.

Bartolomé de Las Casas. *A Short Account of the Destruction of the Indies*. New York: Penguin Classics, 1992. A frank and sometimes disturbing account of the treatment of New World inhabitants by Spanish conquistadores, written by a firsthand observer.

Toby Lester. *The Fourth Part of the World: An Astonishing Epic of Global Discovery, Imperial Ambition, and the Birth of America*. New York: Free Press, 2009. Starting with a famous map printed in 1507, Lester demonstrates how centuries-old European views of the world evolved to encompass the New World.

Buddy Levy. *River of Darkness: Francisco Orellana's Legendary Voyage of Death and Discovery down the Amazon*. New York: Bantam, 2011. Drawing on the accounts of Orellana and his contemporaries, Levy presents a little-known story of the Age of Exploration.

Samuel Eliot Morison. *The Great Explorers: The European Discovery of America*. New York: Oxford University Press USA, 1986. Renowned naval historian Morison presents summaries of many of the important figures in the Age of Exploration, along with personal observations during his travels to see what the explorers saw.

Marco Polo. *The Travels of Marco Polo*. Edited by Peter Harris. New York: Everyman's Library / Random House, 2008. The tales of adventure and travel to distant lands that inspired generations.

Internet Sources

Evan T. Jones. "Alwyn Ruddock: 'John Cabot and the Discovery of America.'" *Historical Research*, April 5, 2007. http://onlinelibrary.wiley.com/doi/10.1111/j.1468-2281.2007.00422.x/full.

Rossella Lorenzi. "Columbus May Not Have Been First to America." Discovery News, May 3, 2012. http://news.discovery.com/history/columbus-cabot-new-world-discovery-120503.html.

Websites

American Journeys: Eyewitness Accounts of Early American Exploration and Settlement (www.americanjourneys.org). This site sponsored by the Wisconsin Historical Society provides digital access to a wide variety of documents and accounts of voyages and explorations from those who led or participated in epic journeys of exploration.

Dictionary of Canadian Biography Online (www.biographi.ca/index-e.html). This site contains interesting sketches of explorers associated with the search for the Northwest Passage and the exploration of modern-day Canada.

Elizabethan Era (www.elizabethan-era.org.uk). This site includes a section on "The Age of Exploration," which includes a selection of short biographies of English, Spanish, and Portuguese explorers, as well as a timeline for the years 1000 to 1600.

European Voyages of Exploration: The Fifteenth and Sixteenth Centuries (www.ucalgary.ca/applied_history/tutor/eurvoya/index.html). This University of Calgary site concentrates on Spanish and Portuguese voyages of discovery and the growth of their respective empires.

History, BBC (www.bbc.co.uk/history). This BBC website covers a wide selection of topics. The "Historic Figures" section includes an alphabetized collection of biographical sketches of British and other explorers from the Age of Exploration, such as John Cabot, Vasco da Gama, and Francis Drake.

Of Maps and Men: In Pursuit of a Northwest Passage (http://libweb5.princeton.edu/visual_materials/maps/websites/northwest-passage/titlepage.htm). This site from Princeton University contains an exhibition of maps, books, photographs, and artwork associated with the early attempts to find the Northwest Passage. It includes summaries of many noteworthy expeditions to the Arctic.

Royal Museums Greenwich (www.rmg.co.uk). Includes a "Sea and Ships" section that has a collection of maps and narratives of several English explorers involved in the Age of Exploration.

Index

Picture Credits

Cover: © Triff/Shutterstock.com

© Art Resource, NY, 35

© Classic Image/Alamy, 16, 33

© DEA/A.C. Cooper/De Agostini/ Getty Images, 29

© DeAgostini/Getty Images, 24, 27, 49, 86

© Gale/Cengage Learning, 20, 37

© Hilary Morgan/Alamy, 65

© Hulton Archive/Getty Images, 60

© Interfoto/Alamy, 32

© Jerónimo Alba/Alamy, 91

Map of Tenochtitlan and the Gulf of Mexico, from 'Praeclara Ferdinadi Cortesii de Nova maris Oceani Hyspania Narratio' by Hernando Cortes (1485-1547) 1524 (colour litho), Spanish School, (16th century)/

Newberry Library, Chicago, Illinois, USA/The Bridgeman Art Library, 43

© Mary Evans Picture Library/Alamy, 63

© MPI/Getty Images, 88

© North Wind Picture Archives/ Alamy, 6 (both), 7 (bottom), 18, 28, 40, 45, 52, 55, 68, 80, 93, 95

© Popperfoto/Getty Images, 73

Royal 12 F.IV, f.135v Diagrammatic world map, c.1175 (vellum)/British Library, London, UK/© British Library Board. All Rights Reserved/ The Bridgeman Art Library, 13

© Stock Montage/Getty Images, 59, 71, 77

© Three Lions/Getty Images, 97

© World History Archive/Alamy, 7 (top), 10

About the Author

Andrew A. Kling became fascinated with other lands and stories of exploration as a youngster. His parents had a huge dictionary that was printed in 1901, which included a center section with colorful maps and flags of countries around the world. The maps and flags inspired him to learn about far-flung lands and forgotten empires. It started a lifelong interest in history, geography, and vexillology (the study of flags). A freelance author, consultant, and bookseller, he also enjoys hockey, travel, music, and spending time with his wife, Laurie, and their famous Norwegian Forest cat, Chester.